ANF

PAID NOV 2003

32

12

12

2

92

P 1992

!

Books by Melvin Harris

Strange to Relate 1 and *2*
Critics' Gaffes (with Ronald Duncan)
Sorry You've Been Duped!
Investigating the Unexplained
Jack the Ripper: The Bloody Truth

THE RIPPER FILE

Melvin Harris

W H ALLEN

First published in Great Britain in 1989 by
W. H. Allen and Co. Plc.
Sekforde House
175/9 St John Street
London EC1V 4LL

Copyright © Melvin Harris 1989

Designed by Ronald Clark

British Library Cataloguing in Publication Data
Harris, Melvin
The Ripper File.
1. London. Murderers: Jack
I. Title
364.1'523'0924

ISBN 1-85227-101-9

Set in Linotype Century Schoolbook by
Poole Typesetting (Wessex) Ltd, Bournemouth.

Printed and bound in Great Britain by
Mackays of Chatham PLC, Letchworth, Herts.

For Maureen M'cushlah; my Lady Macbeth, my Gigi.
What finer combination could one ask?

Contents

All black-and-white illustrations are from the author's own collection, except those on pages 59 and 86, which are reproduced by courtesy of Donald Rumbelow.

Colour Plates

All colour plates, unless otherwise indicated, are from
the author's own collection.

Foreword

Journalists made the running from start to finish. They gave the Ripper legend its bogus start. One journalist penned the first Ripper letters. Others kept the fears at white heat. The very killer was a journalist himself. And for a century other journalists have concocted Ripper hoaxes to fill their columns and pockets.

This book presents a selection of some of the Victorian newspaper reports that helped form and distort public opinion, fuel fears and create myths, myths that still beguile and stupefy over a hundred years on.

These reports lead us inexorably to the fiascos of the centenary year. With those fiascos discarded, new revelations about the real Ripper are presented. Evaluate them carefully. They are provocative – but the truth very often is.

Acknowledgements

My thanks for the cooperative impulses of:
Andy Aliffe; Robin Duff-Cole; Dr Joan Healy
(USA); Francis X. King; Donald Rumbelow;
Leslie Shepard (Dublin); Simon Welfare; Alan
Wesencraft; Richard Whittington-Egan. Spe-
cial thanks to Peter Ainscough and his energe-
tic staff at the Hull Central Library. And to all
librarians, whether tortoises or hares.

Map of the Whitechapel Murders

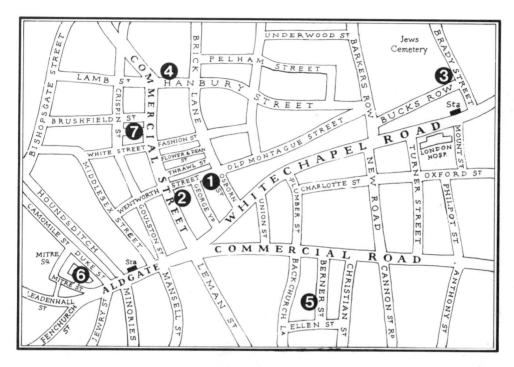

1. Emma Smith
2. Martha Turner
3. Mary Ann Nichols
4. Annie Chapman
5. Elizabeth Stride
6. Catherine Eddowes
7. Mary Kelly

After Kelly's death in November 1888, the *Police News* logged these seven 'Ripper' killings. Was this the right conclusion?

THE MONSTER

1

Hate Strops a Blade

'The Monster' – no other name seemed fitting. Exactly one hundred years before Jack the Ripper's spasm of terror, another unknown menace stalked the streets of London. Women went in constant fear of his dark, warped passions. His slashing knife became part of their daily dreads and suffocating nightmares.

A contemporary newspaper said of him: 'The Monster is now a mischief of more than human magnitude. It is really distressing to walk our streets towards evening. Every woman we meet regards us with mistrust, shrinks from our touch, and expects a poinard to pierce what gallantry and manhood consider as sacred.'

Unlike Jack's, though, none of his victims was killed and mutilated. And unlike Jack, he was captured and brought to trial. His name was Renwick Williams. He was a failed ballet dancer, aged 23, employed as a maker of artificial flowers and at his trial shown to be a man whose hatred of women was once diverted into relatively harmless paths. He was a sexual fetishist. His antagonism was directed at the provocative and at the same time protective clothing worn by women. But the excitement of slashing at garments spilled over into the urge to slash the tempting flesh underneath.

Vice and villainy were rife in the eighteenth century, but Williams's attacks presented the law with a new problem, for the statutes of the time were not precise enough to deal with the crime. Justice Buller termed it '. . . a completely and perfectly new case in itself'. Such a verdict shows how rare and baffling such assaults on women were. They were to remain rare for a whole century, so rare that when the Ripper struck, the *Illustrated London News* had this to say: 'Curiously enough, in the only case that can be said to be any sort of parallel to it, that of Renwick Williams . . . the criminal also escaped justice.' The editor, of course, had in mind the gallows, for The Monster never went scot-free: after two trials Williams was finally convicted and sentenced to two years in Newgate on each of three counts. Then he disappeared from the public eye and passed into obscurity, his case only resurfacing in the following century when similar fetishistic assaults were repeated by another loner and woman-hater. This time, as we shall see, the attacks were destined to lead to four false trails to the real Ripper.

Two other unrelated events were also destined to play their parts in creating these false trails. The first centred round the Turf Frauds Scandal of 1877. Bogus betting syndicates were fleecing gullible members of the public – some of them quite rich. When the police moved in to arrest the con-men behind the schemes they found their efforts thwarted. Someone, somewhere, was tipping off the gang. To police dismay it was discovered that detectives at Scotland Yard, including Chief Inspector William Palmer, were in league with the swindlers. Palmer, along with detectives Meiklejohn and Druscovitch (a Pole), was tried, convicted and sent to prison. From then on any hint of corruption or concealment sent shudders through the police, the public outcry over the 'Druscovitch case' making them ultra-sensitive to anything that gave the appearance of a cover-up at work. Bear this in mind.

The second unrelated factor was the Lipski trial of 1887. Israel Lipski, a young Russian Jew, murdered Miriam Angel by pouring nitric acid down her throat. They both lived in the same slum lodging house in Whitechapel and the evidence against Lipski was overwhelming. Yet some strange popular whim impelled many people to believe Lipski's own defence – that two unknown men had carried out the killing – and consequently when the death sentence was passed it provoked a furious reaction among those who believed him innocent. Lipski's final, full confession left them downcast and bitter and reaction set in. A belief that the Jew was capable of any loathsome act began to fester, and there were plenty of people around eager to help the idea grow. Small wonder, then, that the Jews were ordained to be the primary suspects when the Ripper struck.

Opposite: The Turf Frauds Scandal shakes the police.

BULL'S EYE ON BOBBY.

Mr. Bull (*takes Policeman's lantern*). "THANK YOU. I'LL JUST HAVE A LOOK ROUND MYSELF. STRIKES ME THE PREMISES AIN'T AS CLEAN AS THEY MIGHT BE!"

'Dodo' Henderson's farewell nap.

2
The Cauldron Simmers

After seventeen years in office, Police Commissioner Henderson was dubbed 'The Dodo' by newspaper editor W. T. Stead. Despite such a slur he was a man of immense personal charm and hardly anyone within the Metropolitan Police would level a harsh word at him. But over the years, since his start in 1869, outsiders had gradually come to see him as far too easy-going: they saw police discipline as weak and longed for a more dynamic man to take charge.

Their longings were satisfied when Sir Edmund Henderson was forced to resign, in 1886. The crisis that forced his exit arose when mindless thugs mingled with political demonstrators and began rioting. There was a fracas in Pall Mall and in St James's; in Oxford Street shops were looted. It was a minor outbreak by any standards but that day, 8 February 1886, became known as 'Black Monday', and frightened shopkeepers began to howl for protection. On the following Wednesday, Scotland Yard ordered West End shopkeepers to close up and barricade their premises: a mob was planning an attack under cover of the thick fog – so they thought. It was all runaway rumour, though. There were no attacks and no mobs. The whole sorry affair led to action by Home Secretary Hugh Childers, who censured Henderson so strongly that 'The Dodo' packed his bags and left the Yard for good.

In Henderson's place Childers appointed Sir Charles Warren, a soldier with a formidable reputation. He was humourless and a stern, unbending disciplinarian with a vile temper lurking underneath his cold exterior. While Childers was in office, however, Sir Charles was given a free hand and the terrible temper was kept under control.

The new commissioner entrenched himself by ensuring that five new senior police posts were filled by army officers. Extra inspectors and sergeants were added to the command structure. The magic word from now on was 'discipline'.

Warren's new regime coincided with the problem of how to deal with growing unrest among the unemployed. The industrial and agricultural slump and the unusually bleak winter of 1886 combined to create a mood of bitterness tinged with desperation. Inevitably there was friction between demonstrators and the police. To be fair to Warren, he did notice that 'The roughs congregate with and personate the unemployed and seem bent on mischief,' but the measures he took to head off street scuffles brought him into head-on war with the labour movements of the day. He closed Trafalgar Square to all meetings and demonstrations – but the square ranked as a traditional place for protest, and anger animated the radicals, the socialists, the wretches without work. The battle lines were drawn.

They called it 'Bloody Sunday'. On 13 November 1887, some 20,000 demonstrators tried to enter Trafalgar Square. The police, 4,300 strong, were aided by 300 Grenadier Guards with fixed bayonets and 300 mounted Life Guards carrying sabres. Clash after clash led to casualties all round; among the demonstrators some 300 at least were injured and one man died. 'Amidst the storm he won a prisoner's rest,' wrote William Morris; a martyr's funeral procession was staged; Warren's name was spat out with hate and venom; forgiveness was out of the question. Warren was never allowed to forget 'Bloody Sunday'. The enemies he made that day sniped away at him for the rest of his reign. These were complications he could have well done without, for the new Home Secretary, Charles Matthews, was trouble enough.

Matthews's own private secretary later wrote of him: '. . . he was an exceedingly able lawyer, but quite incapable of dealing with men: he was a regular Gallio in his attitude to Warren's complaints. Later on he quarrelled with [Chief Commissioner] Bradford, and if you couldn't get on with Bradford you could get on with nobody.' Warren's first complaints had been directed against Richard Pennefather, the Receiver of the Police Force, a disagreeable man who had control over police finances but answered only to the Home Secretary. Further complaints all centred around the type of controls imposed on the police by the Home Office: Warren wanted more independence but the Home Office guarded its role jealously.

For the rest of his term in office Warren stayed locked in combat with Matthews and some of the skirmishes were to influence the nature of the coming hunt for the Ripper. Looking ahead, we see that the prime victim of this top-level battle was James Monro, head of the C I D. Warren forced his resignation and replaced him with Robert Anderson – who

'Bloody Sunday' – Warren's blunder.

promptly went on sick leave to Switzerland, on the very eve of the first Ripper killing.

The Warren-Matthews clash weakened a force that would soon need every fragment of its strength for a remorseless hunt. In 1887, though, no one could have guessed that the next year would stretch the police to its limits, and beyond.

Home Secretary Matthews and his 'Bloody Sunday' captives.

Prime Minister Salisbury ushers in turbulence.
Warren keeps order.

POLICE *THE ILLUSTRATED* NEWS

LAW COURTS AND WEEKLY RECORD

No. 1,252.   SATURDAY, FEBRUARY 11, 1888.   Price One Penny.

MURDER AND SUICIDE AT THE EAST END   THE CAMBERLEY POISONING CASE.   ACCIDENT TO A BIRMINGHAM PUGILIST

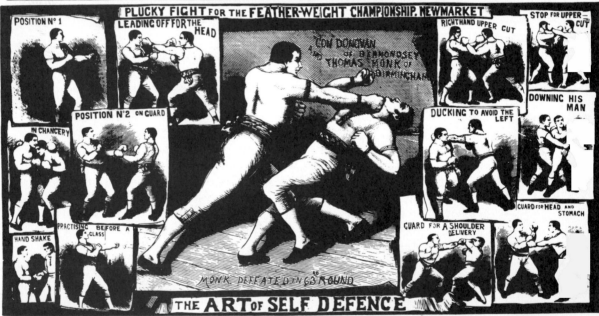

PLUCKY FIGHT FOR THE FEATHER-WEIGHT CHAMPIONSHIP, NEWMARKET

THE ART OF SELF DEFENCE

AWFUL DOMESTIC TRAGEDY IN SALFORD—EIGHT PERSONS DEAD

A death to remember.

3
1888 – the Year of Reckoning

Whitechapel's fateful year opened with the usual street brawls, wife-beatings and petty thefts. Then on Wednesday, 8 February came the first knife murder, when an estranged husband killed his wife then cut his own throat. The weapon used was a boot-finisher's knife; the killer was Jewish and the murder site was in Backchurch Lane. All three factors would later resonate in people's minds.

A very different knifing marred the next month. This time no family hatreds were involved, as *The Illustrated Police News* shows:

On Wednesday morning [28 March] at half-past twelve a desperate attempt to murder a young dressmaker was made at Bow. Screams for help were heard proceeding from Maldmans-street, Burdett-road . . . and a couple of young women rushed up to some police-constables on duty outside *Royal Hotel* and said that a woman was being murdered. The two constables immediately ran to the house . . . and there found a young woman, named Ada Wilson, lying in the passage, bleeding profusely from a fearful wound in the throat. A doctor of the Mile-end-road was instantly sent for, who, after binding up the woman's wounds, sent her to the hospital, where it was ascertained that she was in a most dangerous condition. She, however, so far recovered that she was able to state what had occurred, and gave a description of the would-be murderer.

It appears that she occupies both portions of the house, and was about to retire to rest, when she heard a knock at the door, and upon going there found a total stranger waiting, who demanded money from her, adding that if she did not at once produce the cash she had but a few moments to live. She refused to give the money, and the man drew from his pocket a clasp-knife, with which he stabbed her twice in the throat and immediately made off.

From the details of the man's appearance given by Wilson, the following will be found approximate, if not a certain description of the would-be assassin:– About thirty, height 5ft 6in, face sunburnt, with fair moustache, dressed in dark coat, light trousers, and wideawake hat. Detective-inspectors Wildy and Dillworth have charge of the case . . . It is thought impossible that the injured woman can recover.

As an event, it may later have helped in enlarging the reputation of the Ripper but there really is no discernible connection with the classic murders. Despite this, as recently as 1987, Ada Wilson has been pushed into the spotlights as a possible '... first target of the East End's multiple murderer'.

The first murder that later on gained significance was that of Emma Smith, who died on Wednesday, 4 April. She was described as a 45-year-old widow who acted like a madwoman when drunk. *Police News* reported that:

> On Bank Holiday the deceased left the house in the evening, apparently in good health. She returned home between four and five o'clock the next morning severely injured, and she said she had been shockingly treated by some men ... Deceased further said that she was coming along Osborne-street, Whitechapel, when she was set upon and her money taken from her. On her way to the hospital deceased pointed out the spot, and said she did not know the men, nor could she describe them ... After her admission she slowly sank, and died at nine o'clock on Wednesday morning ... The coroner said that from the medical evidence it was clear that the woman had been barbarously murdered. Such a dastardly assault he had never heard of and it was impossible to imagine a more brutal case.

The crude brutality of the case distances it from the relatively swift throat-cuttings of the Ripper proper, for Emma Smith had been violated with a blunt stick which tore through to her perineum and gave her a lingering, agonising death. Despite the glaring differences, the Smith case was to be named as one of Jack's for many years to come, but in April 1888 it stood as an isolated case. The time was not yet ripe for runaway speculation.

July focused attention on the plight of the hard-pressed in the East End. The match-girls of Bryant and May's went on strike to win better pay and working conditions. Their courageous and moving fight co-incided with the hearings of the House of Lords Sweating Committee. The testimony before that committee disclosed brutal levels of exploitation in the garment trades, and radicals and socialists were quick to harness popular revulsion. A giant march through the East End to Hyde Park was organised. The match-girls were present, so were the leading Reds, ranging from the mildly tinted George Bernard Shaw to the deep-crimson-hued William Morris. Most of the agitation stressed the power latent in strong trades unions but Morris thundered out a resolution of dissent. 'This meeting,' he cried, 'while protesting against the extortion

POLICE ILLUSTRATED NEWS

THE

LAW COURTS AND WEEKLY RECORD.

No. 1,260.   SATURDAY, APRIL 7, 1888.   Price One Penny.

THE GREAT BATTLE BETWEEN SAYERS & HEENAN FARNBOROUGH. 1860.

FACE TO FACE — SAYERS CLAIMS FIRST BLOOD — TOM IN CHANCERY — TOM FLOORED — A BUSTER IN THE RIBS — SAYERS'S ARM INJURED

SAYERS LET FLY HIS LEFT AND KNOCKED HEENAN CLEAN OFF HIS FEET

A FOUL—HEENAN HITS SAYERS WHEN DOWN

HEENAN'S EYES CLOSED

HEENAN FLOORED

SAYERS FORCED TO THE ROPES

TOM PATIENTLY WAITS FOR HEENAN

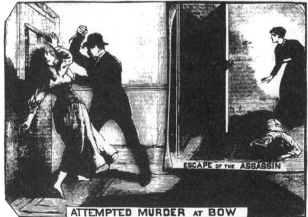

ESCAPE OF THE ASSASSIN

ATTEMPTED MURDER AT BOW

CONFLICT BETWEEN SANDWICH-MEN AT BRIGHTON

Was Ada Wilson involved?

practised under what is known as the sweating system, points out that this is a necessary result of production for profit, and must continue until that is put an end to ... it therefore calls upon all workers to combine in order to bring about the Social Revolution, which will place the means of production and exchange in the hands of the producers.'

Morris was simply shouting into the wind. The anti-sweating protests did little to kindle revolutionary energies; by contrast they did a good deal to strengthen anti-Jewish feelings, for many of the identified sweaters were Jewish. So indeed were many of the exploited, but in the climate of the time people focused on the big men, the whip-wielders, above all.

On 7 August Whitechapel witnessed its second mysterious murder. *Police News* reported:

> John Saunders Reeves, 37, George-yard-buildings, a waterside labourer, deposed that on Tuesday morning he left home at five o'clock to go in search of work. On the first-floor landing he saw a female lying in a pool of blood. She lay on her back, and seemed dead. He at once gave notice to the police. The woman was a perfect stranger to the witness. Her clothes were all disarranged, as if she had had a struggle with some one ...
>
> Dr Timothy Robert Keleene, 28 Brick Lane, stated that he was called to the deceased and found her dead. He examined the body and found thirty-nine punctured wounds. There were no less than nine in the throat and seventeen in the breast. She appeared to have been dead three hours ... He had since made a post mortem examination, and found the left lung penetrated in five places and the right lung in two places. The heart had been penetrated but only in one place otherwise it was quite healthy. The liver was healthy, but penetrated in five places, and the spleen was penetrated in two places. The stomach was penetrated in six places. In the witness's opinion the wounds were not inflicted with the same weapon ...
>
> It now appears that on the night of Bank Holiday there were several soldiers in the neighbourhood ... With these soldiers were the deceased and another woman, the latter being known in the district as 'Megg' and 'Pearly Poll' ... Inspector Reid and the other officers engaged in the case have in no way relaxed their efforts to trace the criminal, and on Monday morning the Inspector, accompanied by 'Pearly Poll' ... proceeded to the Tower, where she was confronted by every non-commissioned officer and private who had leave of absence at the time of the outrage ... 'Can you identify anyone?' she was asked. 'Pearly Poll' exclaimed, with great feminine emphasis, 'He ain't here!'
>
> There have been many visitors to George-yard-buildings with the rather morbid purpose of seeing the place where the deceased was discovered.

Morbid they may have been, but not one of them guessed that they were

30

POLICE THE ILLUSTRATED NEWS
LAW COURTS AND WEEKLY RECORD

No. 1,275.   SATURDAY, JULY 21, 1888.   Price One Penny.

GIRLS ATTACKING A CONSTABLE   ACCIDENTAL DEATH AT THE EAST END   THE DUEL BETWEEN M. FLOQUET & GEN BOULENGER

BRYANT AND MAY'S FIRM AT BOW   A BOOT MAKER'S SWEATING DEN

LOOK HERE TWENTY FOUR HOURS A DAY IN FUTURE

FEVER GERMS

FINISHING BOOTS 2½ PER PAIR

MAKING MATCH BOXES FOR 2¼ PER GROSS

STARVING MATCH MAKERS AT BOW

MATCHGIRLS' STRIKE AT BOW

BOAT ACCIDENT IN MORECAMBE BAY

SERIOUS RIOT IN MANCHESTER

Real grievances – false foes.

THE ILLUSTRATED POLICE NEWS

LAW COURTS AND WEEKLY RECORD

No. 1,279.　　　　　SATURDAY, AUGUST 18, 1888.　　　　　Price One Penny.

RUN OVER AND KILLED　　A CHAMPION BOXER IN THE LION'S DEN　　KILLED ON THE TOBOGGAN

THE HORRIBLE AND MYSTERIOUS MURDER AT GEORGE'S YARD, WHITECHAPEL ROAD

THE MORTUARY

THE UNFORTUNATE VICTIM WAS SEEN DRINKING WITH SOLDIERS

GEORGE YARD

FINDING THE BODY OF THE MURDERED WOMAN ON THE LANDING OF GEORGE BUILDING

ENTRANCE TO GEORGE YARD

VICTIM'S CORSET

STABBED THROUGH

LADY SOMNAMBULIST AT NEW BRIGHTON

L. DONOVAN

FATAL LEAP OF THE CHAMPION DIVER

witnessing the birth of a legend. No one linked the killing with anything similar. No one discerned a pattern, real or imaginary. Within weeks this was all to change. The George Yard victim, Martha Turner, would be seen with new, if myopic, eyes. *Tabram?*

Opposite: The murder of Martha Turner.
Was it the first Ripper killing?

33

POLICE — THE ILLUSTRATED — NEWS

LAW COURTS AND WEEKLY RECORD

SATURDAY, SEPTEMBER 8, 1888.

Price One Penny.

SAD DEATH AT BEDLINGTON

ATTEMPTED MURDER AND SUICIDE IN WALES

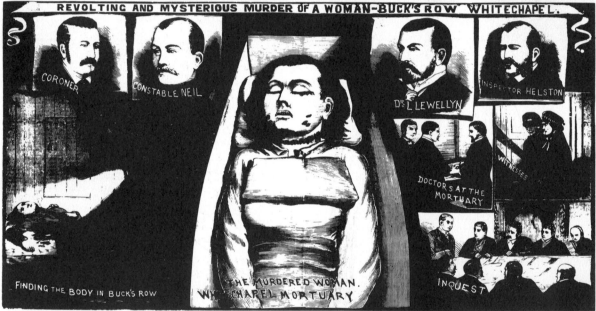

REVOLTING AND MYSTERIOUS MURDER OF A WOMAN—BUCK'S ROW WHITECHAPEL.

CORONER

CONSTABLE NEIL

D.ᵣ LLEWELLYN

INSPECTOR HELSTON

DOCTORS AT THE MORTUARY

WITNESSES

FINDING THE BODY IN BUCK'S ROW

THE MURDERED WOMAN. WHITECHAPEL MORTUARY

INQUEST

AN ENTIRE FAMILY MURDERED

MURDEROUS OUTRAGE AT HANDSWORTH.

4
The Rituals Begin

He struck on the last day of August. In dismal Bucks Row he left the mutilated body of Polly Nichols. It was taunt Number One.

Earlier that day in *The Pall Mall Gazette*, editor W. T. Stead had called for the ousting of the Commissioner of Police. His barbed article said:

> Why does not Lord SALISBURY solve the double difficulty in which he is at present involved by the brilliant stroke of appointing Sir CHARLES WARREN Warden of the Marches on the Upper Zambezi? . . Sir CHARLES WARREN has steadily gone from bad to worse, until he has now succeeded in establishing a condition of things in Scotland-yard which Lord SALIS-BURY may well regard with uneasiness. The resignation of Mr MONRO, the chief of the Criminal Investigation Department, is merely the most conspicuous outward and visible sign of the discontent which Sir CHARLES has created in the force.
>
> Mr MONRO, we hear, is likely to be appointed to be Head of the Third Section of political police . . . But Sir CHARLES WARREN stands in still more urgent need of promotion – away from Scotland-yard. He did admirably at Suakin during his brief term of office. Few pleasanter pictures have ever been seen than that of Sir CHARLES sitting in the market-place at Suakin on the Moslem Sabbath, winning the confidence of the people first by telling stories to the little urchins, and then by holding a kind of democratic levee or audience, which the poorest were free to attend, and where all were free to expose their grievances or to air their complaints. He has done nothing so good since he quit Africa. He will do nothing so good until he returns to Africa again. His disappearance from Scotland-yard would be a great deliverance for the metropolis . . .

The Nichols murder now brought a challenge to Warren far greater than any before. Overnight a new alarm began to sound and links were quickly forged with earlier murders. Could one man, or group of men, be behind *all* the recent killings? *The Times* reported that: 'The police have no theory with respect to the matter, except that a gang of ruffians exists in the neighbourhood, which, blackmailing women of the "unfortunate" class, takes vengeance on those who do not find money for them.

They base that surmise on the fact that within twelve months two other women have been murdered in the district by almost similar means – one as recently as the 6th of August last – and left in the gutter of the street in the early hours of the morning . . .'

Just a week later, the papers were screaming about a fourth murder. *The Pall Mall Gazette* said:

A painful sensation was created all over London today when it was known that early this morning another shocking murder, with even more horrible details than those which characterised others reported recently in the same quarter, was perpetrated in Spitalfields. Again the victim is a woman, again there has been fearful mutilation of the body; and this is the fourth tragedy of the kind in the East-end within a very short period. The first occurred some months ago; the others quite recently. The second case was that in which the body of an 'unfortunate' was found in a lodging-house at George-yard-buildings, Whitechapel, covered with wounds inflicted with a knife. Then came the brutal murder and mutilation of a Mrs Nichols, in Bucks-row, Whitechapel – in the early morning of Friday last and now there is the fourth case which although as stated in the report below, perpetrated in Spitalfields, is nevertheless within a few hundred yards of Bucks-row, Whitechapel. This neighbourhood is today in a state of wild excitement, bordering on panic, for the other cases are fresh in everybody's memory, and nobody has been brought to justice for any one of the crimes . . .

The victim was found in the back yard at No 29 Hanbury-street, Spitalfields . . . by a Mr Davis who lodges in the house. As Mr Davis, who is a market porter, was going to work at about six o'clock, he happened to go into the back yard . . . in the left-hand corner, close to a brick wall, he found the woman lying, horribly mutilated in a pool of blood. Her head was facing the door, the throat was cut and the body ripped . . . When Mr Davis found the woman she was lying on her back . . . The throat was cut open in a fearful manner – so deep in fact, that the murderer, evidently thinking that he had severed the head from the body, tied a handkerchief round it so as to keep it on. It was also found that the body had been ripped open and disembowelled, the heart and abdominal viscera lying by the side. The fiendish work was completed by the murderer tying part of the entrails round the victim's neck.

The Gazette also drew attention to a new feature. A nickname had been slapped on the killer – the strange name 'Leather Apron'. In its editorial *The Gazette* said:

Something like a panic will be occasioned in London to-day by the announcement that another horrible murder has taken place in densely populated Whitechapel. This makes the fourth murder of the same kind,

Too many villains, too few police.

No. 1424.—Vol. 55

THE PENNY

September 15, 1888

ILLUSTRATED PAPER

AND ILLUSTRATED TIMES

REGISTERED AT THE GENERAL POST-OFFICE AS A NEWSPAPER.

London : Printed and Published at the Office, 10, Milford-lane, Strand, in the Parish of St. Clement Danes, in the County of Middlesex, by THOMAS FOX, 10, Milford-lane, Strand, aforesaid.

REAR OF Nº 29, HANBURY ST

Nº 29, HANBURY ST

Mʳˢ A. RICHARDSON
ROUGH PACKING
CASE MAKER.

⊕ WHERE BODY WAS FOUND

ANOTHER MURDER
WHITECHAPEL
ARREST

WE depict the site of the barbarous murder at 29, Hanbury-street, Whitechapel, and the scene in front of the house last Saturday. Succeeding, as it did, several terrible outrages of a similar nature in the same district, this foul assassination of the unfortunate woman, Annie Chapman, alias Sievey, has naturally aroused East London to take sensible precautions to prevent the recurrence of these deplorable murders. A few days after the discovery of the mutilated body of a woman in George-yard last month, a Committee of Safety was formed to assist the Police. Once let every citizen be on the alert to aid the ends of Justice, and such outrages should be stamped out. London needs to be more neighbourly in order to checkmate the criminals in our midst.

SCENE OF THE TERRIBLE MURDER IN HANBURY-STREET, WHITECHAPEL.

POLICE *THE ILLUSTRATED* NEWS

LAW COURTS AND WEEKLY RECORD

No. 1,283.   SATURDAY, SEPTEMBER 15, 1888.   Price One Penny.

THE FOURTH AND MOST HORRIBLE MURDER IN WHITECHAPEL.

29 HANBURY S! WHERE THE CRIME WAS COMMITTED

FINDING THE BODY IN THE BACK YARD.

HOUSE WHERE THE VICTIM WAS LAST SEEN

LATEST SKETCHES OF THE MYSTERIOUS CRIMES OF WHITECHAPEL.

THE FIRST MURDER

OSBORN ST. WHITECHAPLE

CHEAP LODDINGS

CHEAP LODDING HOUSE GEORGE STREET

WHITECHAPEL MORTUARY

THE LAST VICTIM

SECOND MURDER

GEORGE YARD BUILDINGS

GEORGE YARD

LOST

HENRY MURDER

ARRESTED ON SUSPICION

THE THIRD MURDER

BUCK'S ROW

MAKING INQUIRIES AT THE SLAUGHTER HOUSE

WHERE FOURTH BODY WAS FOUND

29 HANBURY S!

SCENE IN A MENACERIE WITH A BLACK LION.

SCENE AT AN IRISH WAKE

Horror at Hanbury Street

EAST END DEPUTATION: 'Another murder, Sir Charles – the fourth in – –'
SIR CHARLES WARREN: 'Why bother me about such a trifle? Still, if something must be done, what do you say, Inspector, to another hour's battalion drill?'

WHITECHAPEL: WARREN ON THE WAR-PATH.

the perpetrator of which has succeeded in escaping the vigilance of the police. The triumphant success with which the metropolitan police have suppressed all political meetings in Trafalgar-square contrasts strangely with their absolute failure to prevent the most brutal kind of murder in Whitechapel. The Criminal Investigation Department under Mr MONRO was so pre-occupied in tracking out the men suspected of meditating political crimes that the ordinary vulgar assassin has a free field in which to indulge his propensities. Whether or not this is the true explanation of the immunity which the Whitechapel murderer enjoys, the fact of that immunity is undoubted. Four poor women, miserable and wretched, have been murdered in the heart of a densely-populated quarter, and not only murdered but mutilated in a peculiarly brutal fashion, and so far the police do not seem to have discovered a single clue to the perpetrator of the crimes.

There is some reason to hope that the latest in this grim and gory series of outrages will supply some evidence as to the identity of the murderer. The knife with which he disembowelled his unfortunate victim and a leathern apron were, it is said, found by the corpse. If so, these are the only traces left by this mysterious criminal . . .

The fact that the police have been freely talking for a week past about a man nicknamed Leather Apron may have led the criminal to leave a leather apron near his victim in order to mislead. He certainly seems to have been capable of such an act of deliberate preparation. The murder perpetrated this morning shows no indication or hurry or of alarm. He seems to have first killed the woman by cutting her throat so deeply as almost to sever her head from her shoulders, then to have disembowelled her, and then to have disposed of the viscera in a fashion recalling stories of Red Indian savagery. A man who was cool enough to do this, and who had time enough to do it, was not likely to leave his leather apron behind him and his knife apparently for no purpose but to serve as a clue. But be this as it may, if the police know of a ruffian who wears a leather apron in Whitechapel whom they have suspected of previous crimes, no time should be lost in ascertaining whether this leather apron, if it really exists, can be identified as his.

This renewed reminder of the potentialities of revolting barbarity which lie latent in man will administer a salutary shock to the complacent optimism which assumes that the progress of civilisation has rendered unnecessary the bolts and bars, social, moral, and legal, which keep the Mr Hyde of humanity from assuming visible shape among us. There certainly seems to be a tolerably realistic impersonification of Mr Hyde at large in Whitechapel. The Savage of Civilisation whom we are raising by the hundred thousand in our slums is quite as capable of bathing his hands in blood as any Sioux who ever scalped a foe. But we should not be surprised if the murderer in the present case should not turn out to be slum bred. The nature of the outrages and the calling of the victims suggest that we have to look out for a man who is animated by that mania of bloodthirsty cruelty which sometimes springs from the unbridled indulgence of the worst passions. We have a plebeian MARQUIS DE SADE at large in Whitechapel. If so, and if he is not promptly apprehended, we shall not have long to wait for another addition to the ghastly catalogue of murder.

There is some reason to hope that the sentiment of horror which the peculiar atrocity of the present crime excites even in the most callous will spur the police into a display of vigorous and intelligent activity. At present the disaffection in the force is so widespread that, unless we are strangely misinformed, the police are thinking more of the possibility of striking against a system which has become intolerable than of over-exerting themselves in the detection of crime. As for the community at large, the panic will probably be confined to the area within which this midnight murderer confines his operations. If, however, a similar crime were now to be committed in the West-end, there would be a panic, the like of which we have not seen in our time. From that, however, we shall probably be spared; but the public will be more or less uneasy as long as the Whitechapel murderer is left at large.

The leather apron found near the body of Annie Chapman was soon dismissed from the reckoning – it belonged to John Richardson, whose mother sold cats' meat at 29 Hanbury Street. But Leather Apron himself was hunted with vigour. Yet who was he? *The Star* had all the answers:

He is five feet four or five inches in height, and wears a dark close-fitting cap. He is thickset, and has an unusually thick neck. His hair is black, and closely clipped, his age being about thirty-eight or forty. He has a small black moustache. The distinguishing feature of costume is a leather apron, which he always wears, and from which he gets his nickname. His expression is sinister, and seems to be full of terror for the women who describe it. His eyes are small and glittering. His lips are usually parted in a grin which is not only not reassuring, but excessively repellent. He is a slipper-maker by trade, but does not work. His business is blackmailing women late at night. A number of men in Whitechapel follow this interest-ing profession. He has never cut anybody, so far as is known, but always carries a leather knife, presumably as sharp as leather knives are wont to be. This knife a number of the women have seen. His name nobody knows, but all are united in the belief that he is a Jew or of Jewish parentage, his face being of a marked Hebrew type. But the most singular characteristic of the man is the universal statement that in moving about he never makes any noise. What he wears on his feet the women do not know, but they agree he moves noiselessly. His uncanny peculiarity to them is that they never see him or know of his presence until he is close by them . . . 'Leather-Apron' never by any chance attacks a man. He runs away on the slightest appearance of rescue. One woman he assailed some time ago boldly prosecuted him for it, and he was sent up for seven days. He has no settled place of residence, but has slept oftenest in a fourpenny lodging-house of the lowest kind in a disreputable lane leading from Brick-lane . . . He ranges all over London and rarely assails the same woman twice. He has lately been seen in Leather-lane . . .

If the ladies had no name to fit him, the police soon felt that *they* had. Sergeant William Thicke (promoted to Inspector – by the press) laid hold of a tremulous Jewish boot-finisher named John Pizer and hauled him off to Leman Street police station. *The Gazette* commented: 'It is thought that if he is not actually implicated in the murder, or murders, he may still be able to throw some light upon the affair, and it is considered probable that he will be charged on suspicion, as without that step being taken the police will be unable to keep him in custody. When this man was apprehended Detective Inspector Thicke took possession of five sharp long bladed knives – which, however, are used by men in Pizer's trade (that of boot-finisher) – and several old hats. With reference to the latter, several women who stated that they were acquainted with the prisoner, alleged he had been in the habit of wearing different hats.'

For a while there was a air of eager expectation, fanned by baseless rumours and crude broadsheets. The killer-Jew had been ensnared. The rope would soon stretch his loathsome neck. Then, on 12 September, *The Gazette* announced:

PIZER SET AT LIBERTY. A half-Spaniard and half-Bulgarian, who gave the name of Emanuel Delbast Violenia, waited on the police yesterday. He stated that he and his wife and children tramped from Manchester to London . . . and took up their abode in one of the lodging houses in Hanbury-street. Early last Saturday morning, walking alone in Hanbury-street, he noticed a man and woman quarrelling in a very excited manner. Violenia distinctly heard the man threaten to kill the woman by sticking a knife into her. They passed on, and Violenia went to his lodging. After the murder he communicated what he had seen to the police. At one o'clock yesterday afternoon Sergeant Thicke, assisted by Inspector Cansby, placed about a dozen men, the greater portion of whom were Jews, in the yard of the Leman-street police-station. Pizer was then brought out and allowed to place himself where he thought proper among the assembled men. He is a man of short stature, with black whiskers and a shaven chin. Violenia was then brought into the yard. Having keenly scutinised all the faces before him, he went up to Pizer and identified him as the man whom he heard threaten a woman on the night of the murder. Subsequently, cross-examination so discredited Violenia's evidence that it was wholly distrusted by the police, and Pizer was set at liberty.

Freedom for Pizer failed to free the minds of the prejudiced who stayed chained to the idea that the murders were the work of a 'dirty, foreign Jew'. 'No Britisher could sink to such depths,' they parroted. Meanwhile, the real killer, every inch an Englishman, sat in his small rooms and smiled mockingly and haughtily. The fools would never understand, even if he pushed an explanation under their stupid noses. One day, perhaps, he'd taunt them with the truth.

5
Printed in Capitals – Gory Red

It was not all frantic hunting. On the day that Pizer was released *The Gazette* said this: 'As an advertisement nothing is so effective as one which is printed in capitals all gory red with human blood. The Whitechapel murder has done great service to the cause of humanity by calling attention to the conditions under which the poor exist in the East-end. There is a very noteworthy article in *The Morning Post* on this subject. Terrible crimes, it is evident, have their uses, like pestilences, earthquakes, and other revelations of unseen forces which in ordinary times slumber unnoticed in our midst.'

The Morning Post article read:

The veil has been drawn aside that covered up the hideous condition in which thousands, tens of thousands, of our fellow creatures live, in this boasted nineteenth century, and in the very heart of the wealthiest, the healthiest, the most civilised city in the world. We have all known for many years that deplorable misery, gross crime, and unspeakable vice – mixed and matted together – lie off the main roads that lead through the industrial quarters of the metropolis. The daily sins, the nightly agonies, the hourly sorrows that haunt and poison and corrupt the ill-fated tenants and sojourners in these homes of degradation and disease have been again and again described with more or less truth and force by our popular writers; but it is when some crime or accident, more than usually horrible, has given vividness and reality to the previously unrealised picture, that we are brought to feel – what our keenest powers failed adequately to conceive before – how parts of our great capital are honeycombed with cells hidden from the light of day, where men are brutalised, women demonised, and children are brought into the world only to be inoculated with corruption, reared in terror, and trained in sin, till punishment and shame overtake them too, and thrust them down to the black depths where their parents lie already lost, or dead to every hope or chance of moral recovery and social rescue. Then comes a terrible crime, bringing a revelation that fills every soul with horror, and makes us ask why sleeps the thunder, and how these things can be?

The answer is in the facts disclosed. Take the latest as a sample of the

London's East-End poor: workhouse 'casuals'.

Poverty and vice at the East End of London.

rest. A wretched back street is crowded with houses of the most miserable class. Nearly all of them are let out in lodgings, of a single room, or part of a room. The house where the murder was committed had no less than six families, all toilers for daily bread, some of questionable honesty or sobriety, and all, we may be sure, contaminated in greater or lesser degree by the vicious surroundings of their distressed home. Loose women have as free run in these abodes as rabbits in a warren. There is a continual coming and going. Precepts of decency are not observed, the standard of propriety is low, the whole moral atmosphere is pestilential. Poverty in its direst form haunts some dwellings, ghastly profligacy defiles others, and this in street after street, alley after alley, cul-de-sac after cul-de-sac, garret after garret and cellar after cellar. Amidst such gross surroundings who can be good? With this atrocious miasma continually brooding over them and settling down among them, who can rise to anything better? Morally these people are not only lost – they are dead and buried.

This is the part of the subject that clamours for immediate consideration, these are miseries that need immediate remedy, these are the lamentable conditions of human existence, which may well tax the wisest counsels and the most philanthropic consideration of the best men and women of the day. Side by side with all the luxury, the ease, the magnificence, and abounding plenty of our vast metropolis, are all these pitiable ground-down people bowed with misery, and steeped in crime. Happily there are here and there, like far-off stars in darkest nights, exceptional instances of honesty. What can be done? How shall the help, the sympathy, the succour of the better circumstanced, the wealthy, and the well-to-do, be brought to bear with sweet reclaiming power among these lost ones?

It is not so much the truncheon of the policemen that is wanted as the wand, magical in its power and healing in its touch, of higher moral ministries – some Christian love shall never be sought by the weary and heavy-laden in vain, where the veriest outcast may knock and feel that there at least are pitying hearts and open hands, the instruments of God in the recovery of man. We take into the reckoning all that is being nobly done for the wretched people, but what we want to urge is that it is not half enough. The saddening sight of pent-up misery which the recent four murders disclose confirm our complaint, that the better-off classes have not yet risen to the height of self-denial and charity which the hardness of the lot of these close-packed, hard-working, much-suffering poor require to enable them to break through the fetters that bind them down and gall their necks till they are fain to let things drift, while they, like Lazarus in his grave, are without the wish or power to rise to anything better.

Since *The Morning Post* was the authentic voice of the Conservative party the radical *Gazette* took pleasure in saying: '. . . a murder sometimes touches a heart indifferent to less violent reminders'. Others were a great deal more abrasive and scathing. What if all the blood-letting had been in the West End? What then? As for Christian charity, what warped thinking lay behind the planning of shelters where the wretched slept in coffin-like boxes under the uplifting slogan 'ARE YOU READY TO DIE?'

The sting of joyless charity.

DETECTIVE-INSPECTOR REID.

A WITNESS FROM THE CLUB.

Dr. BLACKWELL

Dr. PHILLIPS. "HANG THE PAPERS"

MR. WYNNE E. BAXTER. CORONER FOR EAST MIDDLESEX

"SISTERS —!" A RECOGNITION IN THE MORTUARY.

OUTSIDE THE MORTUARY.

6
Inquests and Diversions

September's theories were wayward and confused. Journalists certainly set the muddle in motion by exaggerating the extent of the murders, but Coroner Wynne Baxter gave their errors respectability. At his inquest on Mary Nichols he said, 'We cannot altogether leave unnoticed the fact that the death you have been investigating is one of four presenting many points of similarity, all of which have occurred within the space of about five months, and all within a very short distance of the place where we are sitting.' And that seemed to be an official endorsement – the killer *had* struck four times.

A further myth emerged from the second of Wynne Baxter's inquests, the one on Annie Chapman. His summing-up made the valid point that '. . . the injuries have been made by some one who had considerable anatomical skill and knowledge. There are no meaningless cuts. The organ [the uterus] has been taken by one who knew where to find it, what difficulties he would have to contend against, and how he should use his knife, so as to abstract the organ without injury to it. No unskilled person could have known where to find it, or have recognised it when it was found. For instance, no mere slaughterer of animals could have carried out these operations. It must have been someone accustomed to the post-mortem room. The conclusion that the desire was to possess the missing abdominal organ seems overwhelming.' Yet Wynne Baxter, like the police and everyone else, knew nothing of the caprices of the sexual fetishist, so he looked for a logical explanation and came up with one which was cranky in the extreme.

The coroner framed his striking disclosure in these words:

> . . . we are driven to the deduction that the abstraction of the missing portion of the abdominal viscera was the object . . . It is not necessary to assume lunacy, for it is clear that there is a market for the missing organ. To show this, I must mention a fact which at the same time proves the assistance which publicity and the newspaper press afford in the detection of crime.

POLICE *THE* ILLUSTRATED NEWS

LAW COURTS AND WEEKLY RECORD

SATURDAY, SEPTEMBER 22, 1888.

Price One Penny

"IS HE THE WHITECHAPEL MURDERER?"

READY FOR THE WHITECHAPEL FIEND. WOMEN SECRETLY ARMED.

LATEST DETAILS OF THE WHITECHAPEL MURDERS

ANNIE CHAPMAN BEFORE AND AFTER DEATH

EXCITING SCENE IN BESTOCK AND WOMBWELL'S MENAGERIE

MORE HORRIBLE MYSTERIES.

The horror mounts.

POLICE *THE ILLUSTRATED* NEWS

LAW COURTS AND WEEKLY RECORD

No. 1,285.   SATURDAY, SEPTEMBER 29, 1888.   Price One Penny.

REWARDS FOR BRAVERY—SAVING DROWNING PERSONS

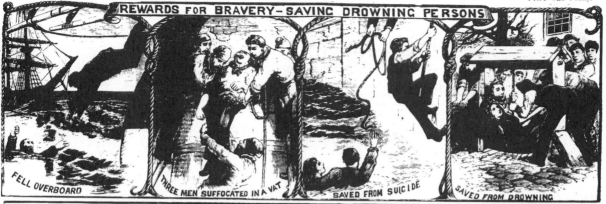

FELL OVERBOARD

THREE MEN SUFFOCATED IN A VAT

SAVED FROM SUICIDE

SAVED FROM DROWNING

THE TERRIBLE TRAGEDY OF ANNIE CHAPMAN'S LIFE. THE LATEST VICTIM OF MYSTERIOUS CRIME.

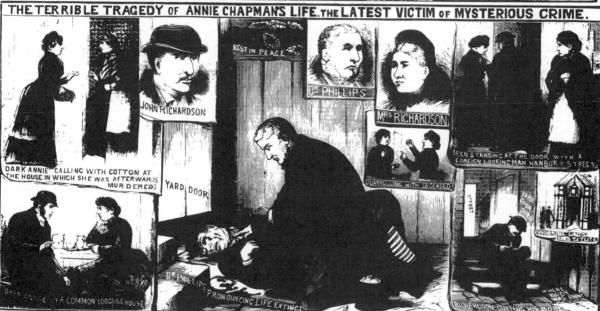

DARK ANNIE CALLING WITH COTTON AT THE HOUSE IN WHICH SHE WAS AFTERWARDS MURDERED

JOHN RICHARDSON

YARD DOOR

REST IN PEACE

Dr PHILLIPS

Mrs RICHARDSON

QUARRELLING WITH DECEASED

SEEN STANDING AT THE DOOR WITH A FOREIGN LOOKING MAN HANBURY STREET

DARK ANNIE IN A COMMON LODGING HOUSE

Dr PHILLIPS PRONOUNCING LIFE EXTINCT

RICHARDSON CUTTING HIS BOOT

WHERE BODY WAS FOUND

CHASE AFTER A MONKEY

FIENDISH MURDER AND MUTILATION AT GATESHEAD.

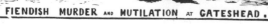

FATALITY AT WEST

Within a few hours of the issue of the morning papers containing a report of the medical evidence given at the last sitting of the court, I received a communication from an officer of one of our great medical schools that they had information which might or might not have a distinct bearing on our inquiry. I attended at the first opportunity, and was informed by the sub-curator of the Pathological Museum that some months ago an American had called on him, and asked him to procure a number of specimens of the organ that was missing in the deceased. He stated his willingness to give £20 apiece for each specimen. He stated that his object was to issue an actual specimen with each copy of a publication on which he was then engaged. He was told that his request was impossible to be complied with, but he still urged his request. It is known that this request was repeated to another institution of a similar character.

Now, is it not possible that the knowledge of this demand may have incited some abandoned wretch to possess himself of a specimen? I need hardly say that I at once communicated my information to the Detective Department at Scotland-yard. By means of the press some further explanation may be forthcoming from America, if not from here. Surely it is not too much even yet to hope that the ingenuity of our detective force will succeed in unearthing this monster. It is not as if there were no clue to the character of the criminal or the cause of his crime. His object is clearly divulged. His anatomical knowledge could only have been obtained by assisting at post-mortems, or by frequenting the post-mortem room.

If the assumption be correct that the man who was talking to the deceased at half-past five was the culprit, he is even more clearly defined. In addition to his former description we should know that he was a foreigner of dark complexion, over forty years of age, a little taller than the deceased, of shabby-genteel appearance, with a brown deer-stalker hat on his head, and a dark coat on his back.

Within days *The Lancet* hit out at Wynne Baxter's fanciful theory. It said:

The revolting tale of the Whitechapel murders has been further embellished by the astounding statements which the coroner deemed fit to make public in his summing up of the case of the unfortunate woman Chapman. The public have supped full of horrors, and now there is added thereto a suggestion which, in spite of its plausibility, is almost too horrible to be credited. It seems, on the face of it, to dispel all previous theories and explanations of a series of crimes which are happily almost unique in our annals. It supplies a motive for the deed, which has been compared to that of Burke and Hare, but which, in fiendish greed and disregard for the sanctity of human life, almost surpasses the villainies of those miscreants. In presence of this suggestion it is futile to discuss any other hypothesis until this has been thoroughly probed. Mr Wynne Baxter did not withhold any of the information which came to him from an unexpected source on the day of the publication of [police surgeon] Mr Phillips's evidence respecting the mutilation of the body. It will be remembered that at his first examination, Mr Phillips did not enter into these details. He acted on his own responsibility in stating only such facts as should enable the coroner's jury to arrive at a correct conclusion as to the cause of death; whilst he took care to inform the police authorities of all those facts which might give them any clue as to the object the murderer had in view, and thus lead to his detection. However, when the coroner insisted upon Mr Phillips being recalled to add these further facts to his previous evidence, he stated that the mutilation of the body was of such a character as could only have been effected by a practised hand. It appears that the abdomen had been entirely laid open; that the intestines, severed from their mesenteric attachments, had been lifted out of the body, and placed by the shoulder of the corpse; whilst from the pelvis to the uterus and its appendages, with the upper portion of the vagina and the posterior two-thirds of the bladder, had been entirely removed. No trace of these parts could be found, and the incisions were cleanly cut, avoiding the rectum, and dividing the vagina low enough to avoid injury to the cervix uteri. Obviously the work was that of an expert – of one, at least, who had such knowledge of anatomical or pathological examinations as to be enabled to secure the pelvis organs with one sweep of a knife, which must therefore, as Mr Phillips pointed out, have been at least five inches long . . .

The theory based on this evidence was coherent enough. It suggested that the murderer, for some purpose or other, whether from a morbid motive or for the sake of gain, had committed the crime for the purpose of possessing himself of the uterus . . . but we must deprecate strongly any tendency to jump at a conclusion in a matter which may admit of another interpretation . . . does it not exceed the bounds of credibility to imagine that he would pay the sum of £20 for every specimen? – whilst the statement that he wished for a large number because *his object was to issue an actual specimen with each copy of a publication on which he was engaged*, is too grotesque and horrible to be for a moment entertained. Nor, indeed, can we imagine that an author of a medical work to be published in America should need to have uteri specially procured for him in England and sent across the Atlantic. The whole tale is almost past belief; and if, as we think, it can be shown to have grown in transmission, it will not only shatter the theory that cupidity was the motive of the crime, but will bring into question the discretion of the officer of the law who could accept such a statement and give it such wide publicity.

Following that, *The Gazette* dug deeper and concluded that the coroner was the victim of a stupid hoax. Their inquiries of the sub-curator of the Pathological Museum disclosed that a complete corpse could be brought for £3 5s; a whole thorax cost a mere five shillings; while fifteen shillings would buy one arm, one leg, one head and neck and one abdomen. These prices referred to pickled dissecting-room subjects. As for the uterus, this could be had for the asking at any post mortem room twelve hours after death! So the hunt for the fanatical American author was over and done with, within a few weeks. But in passing it did nothing to lighten the dark clouds of suspicion hovering over the medical profession.

BRIDGET (newly enlisted servant to set of studios): 'Och! Whirra! It's Jack the Ripper! Police!'

7
Twice – with Impunity!

As the September weeks passed the sensationalists grew restless: in the absence of fresh horrors, something had to be put in their place. The *Police News* tried its ignoble best to fill the gap, first of all with a penny pamphlet called THE WHITECHAPEL MURDERS; *or The Mysteries of the East End. A Thrilling Romance.* Following that, on 22 September it ran an illustrated article headed 'ANOTHER WOMAN STABBED'. Its text read:

> At five minutes after eleven o'clock on Saturday forenoon a man suddenly attacked a woman in Spitalfields-market while she was passing through. After felling her to the ground with a blow, he began kicking her and pulled out a knife. Some women who had collected, having the terrible tragedy that had brought them there still fresh in their minds, on seeing the knife, raised such piercing screams of 'Murder' that they reached the enormous crowds in Hanbury-street. Seeing the immense crowd swarming around him, the man . . . made more furious efforts to reach the woman from whom he had been separated by some persons. . . He, however, threw them on one side, fell upon the woman, knife in hand and inflicted various stabs on her head, cutting her forehead, neck and fingers before he was again pulled off . . . the woman lay motionless – the immense crowd took up the cry of 'Murder' and 'Lynch him'. At this juncture the police arrived. . .

Cunningly, the paper forgot to remind its readers that this report was nothing but an edited version of an article that had already appeared in its issue for 15 September. The original article had made it clear that the knife-man was a *blind* seller of bootlaces and that the stabbed lady was his partner who led him around the streets.

Given the dearth of fresh London horrors, attention turned to the provinces, as *The Gazette* shows. On 24 September 1888 it said:

> The murder and mutilation of a woman near Gateshead yesterday morning will revive in the provinces, the horror which was beginning to die out in London. The coroner in summing up the evidence in the case of the woman NICHOLLS [*sic*] went through once more the points of suspicious similarity in the four Whitechapel murders. In some respects the Gateshead murder

is said to closely resemble them; and already the people in the neighbour-hood have begun, it seems, to be haunted by the idea that the murderous maniac of Whitechapel may have made his way to the North of England. The idea is natural, but improbable. What is far more likely is that the Birtley murder is not a repetition, but a reflex, of the Whitechapel ones. It is one of the inevitable results of publicity to spread an epidemic. Just as the news of one suicide often leads to another, so the publication of the details of one murder often leads to their repetition in another murder. Reading of means to do ill deeds makes ill deeds done. This, we suppose, was one of the motives which led the Whitechapel doctor to suppress so long as he could the results of his post-mortem. The coroner ultimately insisted on the full facts being stated, and in view of the many countervail-ing advantages which result from publicity, it is impossible to blame either the coroner for eliciting or the press for printing the particulars of the Whitechapel horrors. But news is one thing; literature is another. And if there is going to be either an epidemic, or a panic, of murder in the North of England, it will be strange if some of the public indignation is not visited upon the newspapers which set their readers to sup upon 'Newgate Calenders' and tales of crime.

While the press fished around for copy, an immature and irresponsible journalist decided to manufacture some of his own in the form of a mocking letter supposed to be penned by the killer himself. It was dated 25 September but not posted until the 27th and it was not sent to the police or any specific paper but to the Central News Office in Fleet Street. In that way it was meant as a present to all journalists. As it happened, it proved a fantastic boon, for the letter not only gave a name to the killer but it arrived just before he struck again in spectacular fashion. This time it was twice in one night and this time the killings could be bill-posted along with the newly bestowed name of their perpetrator – JACK THE RIPPER.

The double event of 30 September opened in narrow, badly lit Berner Street, a turning off Commercial Road. One murder took place just yards away from the walls of the International Working Men's Educa-tion Society, a body with a largely Jewish membership. The corpse was discovered by the club steward on his return home with his horse and cart. As reported in *The Gazette*:

> He turned into the gateway, when he observed some object lying in his way . . . Unable to see clearly what it was, he struck a match and found that it was a woman. He thought at first she was drunk, and went into the club. Some of the members went out with him and struck another light, and were horrified to find the woman's head nearly severed from her body and blood

London: Printed and Published at the Office, 10, Milford-lane, Strand, in the Parish of St. Clement Danes, in the County of Middlesex, by Thomas Fox, 10, Milford-lane, Strand, aforesaid.

THE DISCOVERY IN MITRE SQUARE

LONDON'S REIGN OF TERROR: SCENES OF SUNDAY MORNING'S MURDERS IN THE EAST-END.

POLICE ~ THE ILLUSTRATED ~ NEWS

LAW COURTS AND WEEKLY RECORD

MORTUARY

THE BERNER ST VICTIM.

INSPECTOR REID

INQUEST ON FIFTH VICTIM AT ST GEORGES IN THE EAST.

TWO MORE WHITECHAPEL HORRORS. WHEN WILL THE MURDERER BE CAPTURED?

BACK OF BERNER STREET

POLICE CONSTABLE WATKINS SIGNALLING FOR ASSISTANCE

MITRE SQUARE ALDGATE — THE FATAL SPOT

THE SCENE ON SUNDAY IN BERNER STREET

FINDING THE BODY IN MITRE SQUARE

EXTERIOR OF THE GATE

THE FIFTH VICTIM OF TH WHITECHAPEL FIEND.

FINDING THE MUTILATED BODY.

streaming down the gutter. The police were summoned, and the poor creature was borne to the St George's dead-house. The corpse was still warm, and in the opinion of the medical experts . . . the deed of blood must have been done not many minutes before. The probability seems to be that the murderer was interrupted by the arrival of the cart, and that he made his escape unobserved, under the shelter of the darkness, which was almost total at the spot . . . The body has been identified as that of a woman named Elizabeth Stride . . .

An interrupted ritual was anathema to the killer. He sped swiftly through the back streets to a new place of appointment – this time on the territory of the City of London police. *The Gazette* again:

At the precise moment that the police were gathering about the place of slaughter in Berner-street, another and more horrible shambles was being provided for their inspection scarcely half a mile away. Shortly before two o'clock Police-Constable Watkins (No. 881), of the City Police, was going round his beat, when, turning his lantern upon the darkest corner of Mitre-square, Aldgate, he saw the body of a woman, apparently lifeless, in a pool of blood. He at once blew his whistle, and several persons being attracted to the spot, he despatched messengers for medical and police aid. Inspector Collard, who was in command at the time at Bishopsgate police-station, but a short distance off, quickly arrived, followed a few moments after by Mr G. W. Sequeira, surgeon, of 35 Jewry-street, and Dr Gordon Brown, the divisional police doctor of Finsbury-circus. Chief Superintendent Major Smith, Superintendent Foster, Inspector McWilliams, and Inspector Collard immediately organised a 'scouting' brigade, to detect and arrest any suspicious looking character, but no one was taken into custody.

In the meantime, Dr Sequeira and Dr Gordon Brown made an examination of the body. The sight was a most shocking one. The woman's throat had been cut from the left side, the knife severing the main artery and other parts of the neck. Blood had flowed freely, both from the neck and body, on the pavement. Apparently, the weapon had been thrust into the upper part of the abdomen and drawn completely down, ripping open the body, and, in addition, both thighs had been cut across. The intestines had been torn from the body, and some of them lodged in the wound on the right side of the neck. The woman was lying on her back, with her head to the south-west corner, and her feet towards the carriage way, her clothes being thrown up on to her chest. Both hands outstretched by her side.

News of these fresh horrors swept throught the East End, and a *Gazette* reporter wrote this of the reaction:

On approaching the scene of the murders yesterday morning it was easy to see, no nearer than a mile away, that something unusual was in the air.

POLICE *THE* ILLUSTRATED NEWS
LAW COURTS AND WEEKLY RECORD

& SONS PORK BUTCHERS.

ARREST IN WHITECHAPEL OF
A MAN IN WOMANS CLOTHING.

THE WHITECHAPEL MYSTERY.

THE MITRE SQUARE VICTIM, BEFORE & AFTER DEATH.

KITCHEN OF A DOSS HOUSE
IN WHITECHAPEL.

SKETCHES OF THE FIENDISH WORK OF THE MONSTER OF WHITECHAPEL. HIS SIX CRIMES.

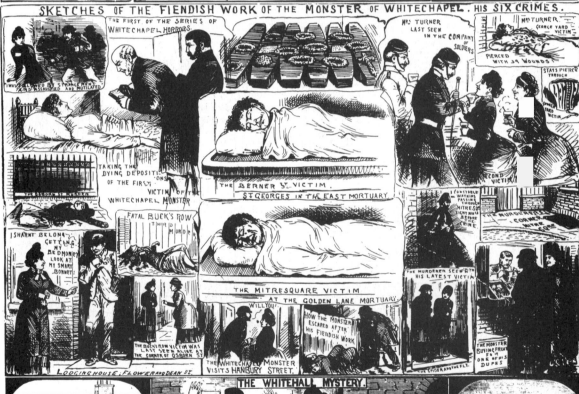

THE FIRST OF THE SERIES OF WHITECHAPEL HORRORS.

I WAS FOLLOWED BY STRANGE MEN AND ASSAULTED AND MUTILATED

TAKING THE DYING DEPOSITIONS OF THE FIRST VICTIM OF THE WHITECHAPEL MONSTER

THE GEORGE ST MURDER

I SHARNT BELONG GETTING MY BED MONEY LOOK AT MY SMART BONNET!

FATAL BUCK'S ROW THIRD MURDER

THE BUCKS ROW VICTIM WAS LAST SEEN ALIVE AT THE CORNER OF OSBORN ST

LODGING HOUSE, FLOWER AND DEAN ST.

THE BERNER ST VICTIM.
ST GEORGES IN THE EAST MORTUARY

THE MITRE SQUARE VICTIM
AT THE GOLDEN LANE MORTUARY.

WILL YOU!

HOW THE MONSTER ESCAPED AFTER HIS FIENDISH WORK

THE WHITECHAPEL MONSTER VISITS HANBURY STREET.

MRS TURNER LAST SEEN IN THE COMPANY OF SOLDIERS

MRS TURNER GEORGE YARD VICTIM

PIERCED WITH 39 WOUNDS

STAYS PIERCED THROUGH

GEORGE YARD VICTIM

SECOND VICTIM

I CONSTABLE WATKINS PASSING THROUGH MITRE SQ EIGHT MINUTES BEFORE THE CRIME.

THE MURDERER CORNER MITRE SQ.

THE MURDERER SEEN WITH HIS LATEST VICTIM

THE SPIDER AND THE FLY.

THE MONSTER BUYING FRUIT FOR ONE OF HIS DUPES

THE WHITEHALL MYSTERY.

MILLBANK STREET MORTUARY

DISCOVERING THE MUTILATED TRUNK.

EXTERIOR OF WORKS, CANNO'

THE ILLUSTRATED POLICE NEWS
LAW COURTS AND WEEKLY RECORD

No. 1,289.   SATURDAY, OCTOBER 27, 1888.   Price One Penny.

The name 'Jack the Ripper' sweeps the land.

Along all the main thoroughfares a constant stream of passengers, all impelled by the same motive of horrified curiosity, were rolling towards the district. The scanty details which had then transpired were eagerly passed from mouth to mouth. There was but one topic of conversation. The few acres of streets and houses between Mitre-square and Berner-street seemed to be a goal for which all London was making.

At the actual places the scene was naturally even more remarkable. The two adits to Mitre-square were blocked by hundreds, and during part of the day thousands, of persons struggling for a place where they could look on the fatal spot. A bar of police kept the crowd outside the square. As one of these was heard inquiring, 'What did they want to see? The body has been taken away long ago, and even the blood was all washed away.' However, the barren satisfaction of trying to peer round the fatal corner continued to be enjoyed by long lines of men, women, and children, going and returning. After a glance at one place, the spectators hurried away to the other. From Commercial-road, Berner-street seemed a sea of heads from end to end. At both places on the fringe of the crowd the opportunity for business was seized by costers with barrows of nuts and fruit, a shop even opened for the purpose in Mitre-street. One remark, overheard in Commercial-road, was in this strain: 'Well, it brings some trade down this end anyway.'

At nightfall the stream ran the other way. There seemed to be an exodus of disreputability from the East. Along the two great avenues leading westward the miserable creatures who apparently have most to fear from the mysterious criminal seemed to be migrating to a safer and better-lit quarter of the metropolis. The noisy groups fleeing before the approaching terrors of night were conspicuous among the better-dressed wayfarers in Holborn and the Strand.

Unknown to the sightseers, a second message signed 'Jack the Ripper' was then being drafted. The postcard carrying this message was sent, like the letter, to the Central News Office and it pretended to be a first-hand comment on the two murders. Note though, that it was posted on 1 October, when most of the details of the killings were well known to anyone involved in the newspaper world. With time, this fact would be forgotten and a myth would arise that the killer had boasted of his deeds *immediately* after the killings, before the news was widespread.

Within days the whole country was speaking of the killer as 'Jack the Ripper', for the police had issued hundreds of posters carrying clear, full-sized facsimilies of both letter and postcard. The poster appealed for anyone who recognised the handwriting to come forward and say so. There was a massive response – all quite useless. And then began the stream of time-wasting letters, all signed with the killer's new name.

The whole sordid drama of murder and guilt,
The steel that strikes home, and the blood that is spilt.

POLICE THE ILLUSTRATED NEWS

LAW COURTS AND WEEKLY RECORD

No. 1,288.   SATURDAY, OCTOBER 20, 1888.   Price One Penny.

INCIDENTS RELATING TO THE EAST END MURDERS

THE HISTORY OF THE LAST VICTIMS OF THE MYSTERIOUS MONSTER OF THE EAST-END.

SKETCHES OF THE WHITEHALL MYSTERY.

IDENTIFYING A MISSING LIMB.   TAKING THE REMAINS TO THE MORTUARY.

More suspects, more theories.

8
Blind Man's Buff

Was the Ripper a woman? Only the Reverend Sydney Godolphin Osborne would dare suggest such a thing at the time. Yet later none other than Conan Doyle was prepared to share this view, and later still William Stewart wrote a book based on the idea. But in 1888 few gave the notion a second thought: after all, there were so many other enticing ideas to enthuse over. *The Gazette*, in October, itemised some as follows:

PARDON TO ACCOMPLICES – There is a theory that the murderer must be known to some one who has withheld information in expectation of reward. He is now afraid. Promise him a pardon.

BLOODHOUNDS – They ran Fish, the Blackburn barber, to earth, and it is suggested that they should be tried in Whitechapel. Mr Percy Lindley, a breeder of bloodhounds, says that as all trace of the scent has been trodden out, they would be useless at present, but suggests that a pair of these dogs should be kept for a time at one of the police head-quarters, ready for immediate use.

EVERY ONE TO REPORT TO THE POLICE BEFORE GOING TO BED – Another idea is to draw a line round the area of the murders, constitute a number of temporary police-stations, and make every man living in the area report himself before going to bed.

HE COMES FROM TEXAS – *The Daily News* says that some time ago Texas was horrified by a similar series of murders. They have ceased. Perhaps the murderer has crossed the Atlantic and renewed his experiments in Whitechapel.

A FANATICAL VIVISECTIONIST – A surgical theory comes from Paris that the murderer is a fanatical vivisectionist and disciple of Haeckel, the German naturalist, who followed in the steps of Darwin in studying the origin of species, and who advanced some startling ideas that have not yet been established.

POLICEMEN AS WOMEN – that policemen should disguise themselves as women, and act as decoys. The policemen say they have beards and bass voices.

THE WORK OF A RELIGIOUS MANIAC – The murders point to one individual, and that individual insane. Not necessary an escaped, or even as yet recognised lunatic. He may be an earnest religionist with a delusion that he has a mission from above to extirpate vice by assassination. And he has selected his victims from a class which contributes pretty largely to the factorship of immorality and sin.

THE JEKYLL AND HYDE THEORY – The murderer lives two lives, and inhabits two houses and two sets of rooms.

OBEDIENCE TO THE TALMUD – Among certain fanatical Jews there exists a superstition to the effect that if a Jew became intimate with a Christian woman he would atone for his offence by slaying and mutilating the object of his passion. Sundry passages of the Talmud are said to sanction this form of atonement.

THIS IS AN ENGLISH DETECTIVE. YOU MAY KNOW HIM ANYWHERE BY HIS REGULATION BOOTS.

'The police should dress as women.' A bold idea, but it had its problems!

POLICE *THE ILLUSTRATED* NEWS

LAW COURTS AND WEEKLY RECORD

SCENES AND INCIDENTS OF THE MYSTERY OF THE EAST END.

A DISGUISED DETECTIVE READY FOR THE WHITECHAPEL MONSTER.

I'M JACK THE RIPPER!

LADY FRIGHTENED TO DEATH.

SHADOWED BY A DETECTIVE DISGUISED AS A FEMALE.

HARLOW HOUSE. MILE END ROAD. FEMALE OUTCAST SHELTER.

HOW TO PREVENT MURDER. THE WHITECHAPEL MONSTER OUTWITTED.

JUSTICE IS BLIND!

HARLOW HOUSE FEMALE OUTCASTS' SHELTER.

HOMELESS FEMALES TUCKED IN FOR THE NIGHT.

THE ALLEGED MURDER AT HUNTINGDON.

A POLICEMAN STABBED AT WALTHAMSTOW.

BARBAROUS CRUELTY.

ATTEMPTED MURDER OF A BROTHER AT WORKSOP.

AVENGING LIPSKI – That some of Lipski's compatriots have turned wholesale murderers for the purpose of showing that the police are mostly fools.

The Gazette itself remained faithful to W. T. Stead's political line, as this quote from 2 October shows:

Mrs Fenwick Miller's letter in *The Daily News* is clever and timely. As long as Sir Peter Edlin deems it the first duty of a judge to condemn men who commit brutal outrages on women to merely nominal punishment, it is idle to expect that the ruffianly fraternity will regard women as other than fair game. Mrs Miller's letter suggests yet another theory of the murders – to wit, that the scientific sociologist, to whom we attributed them some time ago, wished to bring forcibly before the public mind, the natural corollary of the impunity with which the maiming of women is regarded by the magistrates and judges. 'Week by week and month by month women are kicked, beaten, jumped on till they are crushed, chopped, stabbed, seamed with vitriol, bitten, eviscerated with red-hot pokers, and deliberately set on fire – and this sort of outrage, if the woman dies is called "manslaughter"; if she lives it is "common assault".' Then arose the sociologist who wishes to carry the experiment one step further, and these murders are the result.

The Gazette also drew attention to a theory which harmonised to some extent with Stead's.

The Standard thinks that the Whitechapel murders point to the 'incalculable cunning of mania'. But, curiously, it is just this element of cunning which decides the best expert opinion against the maniac theory. The murders might otherwise, says Dr Savage ... have been done by an epileptic, 'but I should not have expected such skilful concealment'. As for the theory of homicidal mania other than such as might be caused by epilepsy, Dr Savage says: – 'I do not think that any epileptic or drunken maniac would have so cunningly selected his victims and avoided detection, and the failure to identify anyone is in favour of there being only one agent. A mere lust for blood would not have been satisfied by the selection of victims. The skill with which the murders were perpetrated and the skill of the mutilation point to someone with some anatomical knowledge. The cunning of the evasion, the ferocity of the crimes, the special selection of the victims, seem to me to depend either on a fiendishly criminal revenge, or else upon some fully organised delusion of persecution or world-regeneration.'

Other papers, including *The Times*, were then running dubious stories which reflected badly on the Jews, hinting that Jewish superstitions could well be behind the murders. The most potent of these stories involved a murder in Galicia, said to have been done by Moses Ritter, a Jewish rapist. *The Gazette* reacted with justifiable anger: 'We hope that Dr Hermann Adler [Chief Rabbi] will lose no time in publishing a conclusive refutation of the absurd story telegraphed to *The Times* from Vienna as to the sanction alleged to be given by the Talmud to the crimes of the Whitechapel murderer. We utterly refuse to believe for a single moment that the Talmud in any of its isolated texts contains any words

Dr Hermann Adler
(Chief Rabbi)

which by any possibility could be construed as amounting to a promise to a Jew who has broken the seventh commandment of absolution if he also breaks the sixth. The feeling against the Jews is quite strong enough in the East-end already without adding to it this groundless calumny.'

Chief Rabbi Adler did, in fact, protest at once and pointed out that: '. . . no one knows what an excited mob is capable of believing against any class which differs from the mob majority by well-marked characteristics. Many English and Irish workpeople in the East End are inflamed against the immigrant Jews by the competition for work and houses, by the stories of the sweaters and the sweated. If these illogical and ignorant minds should come to believe in the report heedlessly spread by a writer who is not quite just nor well informed himself, the results might be terrible.'

Dr Adler was justified in his fears. The Mitre Square killing *was* now being linked with a chalked message left on the entrance wall of a building in Goulston Street. Beneath the message was found a blood-stained piece of an apron belonging to the victim, Catherine Eddowes, and everyone concluded that the two were connected. What did the message say? On that there was no complete agreement – the text printed in one paper differed from that printed in another – but what they were all agreed on was that the message had involved the Jews.

The version distributed by the Central News Agency said:

> A startling fact has just come to light. After killing Katherine [*sic*] Eddowes in Mitre-square, the murderer, it is now known, walked to Goulston-street, where he threw away the piece of the deceased woman's apron upon which he had wiped his hands and knife. Within a few feet of this spot he had written upon the wall, 'The Jews shall not be blamed for nothing.' Most unfortunately one of the police officers gave orders for this writing to be immediately sponged out, probably with a view of stifling the morbid curiosity which it would certainly have aroused.

On learning of the police action *The Gazette* ran this comment:

> Until this year English people have failed to understand how it is that in Hungary, Roumania, and in Russia popular outbreaks of savage ferocity from time to time take place against the Jews. This year we have unfortunately no difficulty whatever in realising how easily popular passion can be excited against the sons of Israel. We have not yet come to Jew-baiting in East London. But when we read this morning that Sir Charles Warren thought it better to destroy a clue to the Whitechapel murderer rather than to allow an inscription implicating the Jews in the murder to remain on a wall till daylight for fear of an outbreak, we understand how near we are to such a peril. 'So real were the apprehensions of the police authorities in this connection that on the Sunday night of the murders the chief police stations in the East-end were reinforced by fifty constables each.' Unfortunately the action of Sir Charles Warren in destroying evidence that might seem to have implicated the Jews is just the kind of thing to excite popular feeling far more bitterly against the Jews than the inscription itself.

Regrettably, the whispers about ritual murders were hard to quell, indeed they were given added strength by fresh stories from Eastern Europe. *Police News* ran such a story under the heading A NEW LIGHT ON THE CRIMES. The text ran:

> The Vienna correspondent of *The Standard* states that Dr Bloch, a member of the Austrian Reichsrath for the Galician constituency of

Kokomea, has called his attention to certain facts which may throw a new light on the Whitechapel murders, and perhaps afford some assistance in tracing the murderer. In various German criminal codes . . . punishments are prescribed for the mutilation of female corpses with the object of making from the uterus and other organs the so-called 'diebelichter' or 'schlafelichter', respectively 'thieves' candles' or 'soporific candles'. According to an old superstitution, still rife in various parts of Germany, the light from such candles will throw those upon whom it falls into the deepest slumbers, and they may, consequently, become a valuable instrument to those of the thieving profession. Hence arose their name . . . They played an important part in the trials of robber bands at Odenwald and in Westphalia, in the years 1812 and 1841 respectively. The 'schlafelichter' were heard of too, at the trial of the notorious German robber Theodor Unger . . . who was executed at Magdeburg, in 1810. It was on that occasion discovered that a regular manufactory had been established by gangs of thieves for the production of such candles. That this superstition has survived among German thieves to the present day was proved by a case tried at Blala, in Galicia as recently as 1875. In this the body of a woman had been found mutilated in precisely the same way as were the victims of the Whitechapel murderer . . .

The paper then went on to add that these gruesome candles had also been introduced into evidence at the trial of the Jew, Moses Ritter.

Even *The Gazette* was lured into printing a similar story, though without any specific anti-Jewish overtones. It read:

A WHITECHAPEL MURDER IN RUSSIA. A brutal murder, writes our St Petersburg correspondent, has just been committed in the south of Russia which bears one or two points of resemblance to the Whitechapel murders, and is also one of a whole class of similar outrages not confined to any one locality. The details may not prove uninteresting to the readers of *The Pall Mall Gazette*. The motive of these crimes, we may say at once, is superstition. A peasant girl was found lying dead in a wood near Graivoron [government of Kursk], with evident signs of having been brutally murdered. Moreover certain portions of the body were missing. For several days all efforts to find the murderers were unavailing. No one was even suspected. Soon afterwards, however, a robbery was committed in the village, and suspicion fell on two peasants who were at once arrested. On their rooms being searched a handkerchief was found in which something in the nature of tallow – extracted from human fat – was carefully rolled up. The mother of the murdered girl recognised the handkerchief as her daughter's, and the mystery was soon cleared up. The prisoners at once confessed and related the history of the crime in all its details. The hand of a corpse, or even the finger, or a candle made of human fat, is firmly believed by the lower classes throughout the length and breadth of Russia to render the thief who possesses it safe from detection; and as there are many thieves in Russia desirous of pursuing their occupations with impunity, the demand for these objects is considerable. These two peasants resolved to procure some 'magic candles' before entering on a series of predatory expeditions. They at first fixed on a peasant as their victim, but when they came to where he was working alone they found him with an axe in his hand, and knowing him to be a strong man they thought it wise to choose another victim. An abnormally stout priest was accordingly fixed upon, but when they called on him he was away, administering the sacraments to a dying man. They then espied this healthy peasant girl, followed her to the wood, despatched her, and removed certain parts of the body, which they afterwards boiled. They are now under an unusually strong guard and their trial will take place in a few weeks.

People reading these pieces were by now aware that the Ripper had removed the wombs of at last two of his victims, so they were not slow in making morbid connections. No one at that stage, though, had pointed to another group interested in acquiring potent segments of a woman's body. No one had yet seriously thought of the bizarre ideas embraced by followers of black magic.

9
Strange Ripples

A butchered woman's body was found in Westminster. Parts of a female corpse were found in Guildford. A severed arm turned up in Lambeth. Had the Ripper suddenly become mobile and shifted his territory? Were his techniques being altered? These were some of the problems the police had to face in the first week of October 1888. It was a time-consuming diversion, unconnected with the Ripper, but it all added to the atmosphere of terror.

Other diversions were created by a spate of stupid Ripper impersonators. *Police News* noted the craze, saying: 'It is becoming quite the thing among the residuum to personate "Jack the Ripper". The corner-man has at last found a change of occupation. Instead of making our streets hideous by violent and disorderly conduct, he goes about the less frequented thoroughfares with a large knife which he brandishes in the face of defenceless women. It is hard to say which is the more objectionable proceeding. It is clear, however, that this new form of idiocy must be sternly repressed. It is satisfactory to notice that a number of these cowardly brutes have been promptly handed over to the police. If this continues to be done, and if the magistrates give them no quarter, they will soon be giving up their new game.'

There were others, far from sinister, who were also skilled at time-wasting. They came from the psychic camp. Perhaps they had been spurred into action by the sly column in *The Gazette* which read: 'There is some sense, though not much importance, in the suggestion that the Whitechapel murders afford the practitioners of occult science (or religion) an unexampled opportunity to prove and advertise the genuineness of their pretensions. If spiritualists, clairvoyants, and thought-readers all 'lie low and say nuffin', we may at least conclude that, whatever spirits may be present at their seances, public spirit is notably absent. Interviews with Carlyle and Shakespeare may be all very interesting, but a short conversation with one of the six spirits so recently sent to their long abode. . . would for practical purposes be worth more than a volume of trans-Stygian Carlylese. Clairvoyants, even if the mere local influence be insufficient to unseal their spiritual eyes, might set to work upon "Jack the Ripper's" letter and determine whether it be genuine or a hoax. Why does the Society for Psychical Research stand ingloriously idle?'

As if in answer to such a challenge, psychic revelations started to pour in. *Police News* gave the following information: 'A strange statement bearing upon the Whitechapel tragedies was made to the Cardiff police on Monday by a respectable-looking elderly woman, who stated that she was a Spiritualist, and, in company with five others, held a seance on Saturday night. They summoned the spirit of Elizabeth Stride, and after some delay the spirit came, and in answer to questions, stated that her murderer was a middle-aged man, whose name she mentioned, and who resided at a given number in Commercial-road, or Street, Whitechapel, and who belonged to a gang of twelve. At another spiritualistic seance held at Bolton on Tuesday a medium claims to have had revealed the Whitechapel murderer. She describes him as having the appearance of a farmer, dressed like a navvy, with a strap round his waist, and peculiar pockets. He wears a dark moustache and bears scars behind the ears and other places. He will, says the medium, be caught in the act of committing another murder.'

On the more earthly plane, Jack was rapidly identified as an American, an Austrian and a Malayan. *Police News* reported that: 'A news agency has received a telegram from New York with respect to a statement alleged to have been made in that city by an English sailor bearing the peculiar name of Dodge. The statement is that he arrived in London from China on the 13th of August by the steamship *Glenorchy*, that he met at the Queen's Music-hall, Poplar, a Malay cook, and that the Malay said he had been robbed by a woman of bad character, and unless he found the woman and recovered his money he would murder and mutilate every Whitechapel woman he met . . . A Reuter's telegram says *The New York Herald* declares that Dodge said that he knew the street where the Malay stayed, but that he would not divulge the name until he learned what chance there was of a reward.'

In another report the paper said: 'Superintendent Farmer, of the River Tyne Police, has received information which, it is considered, may form a clue to the Whitechapel murders. An Austrian seaman signed articles on board a Faversham vessel in the Tyne on Saturday, and sailed for a

Sir Charles braves the bloodhounds.

French port. Afterwards it was found that his signature corresponded with the facsimile letters signed "Jack the Ripper", and that the description of the man also corresponded with that of the Whitechapel murderer circulated by the Metropolitan police.'

As light relief, many of the papers took pleasure in reporting the fact that the dignified Sir Charles Warren had agreed to act as the frightened quarry in a trial of bloodhounds to be staged in Hyde Park. At the trials

Sir Charles mesmerised by will-o'-the-wisp.

Was the strange visitor behind the 'Eddowes kidney' hoax?

everyone, including Sir Charles, seemed impressed by the frisky hounds and there were high hopes that they would prove their mettle when set on Jack's trail. But any humour was superseded by nausea when readers reflected on this passage in *Police News*: 'Mr Lusk, the president of the Whitechapel Vigilance Committee, has received by parcel post a cardboard box containing what has been pronounced by a competent medical authority to be half of the left kidney of an adult human being, and a letter dated from "Hell", stating, with a literate brutality, that the half-kidney was . . . that taken from Catherine Eddowes, and that the other half had been fried and eaten by the writer. The box, with its contents, has been handed over to the detectives at the Leman-street police-station.'

No one doubted that the police were following up every possible clue, including the decomposing kidney, but in October there were many who doubted that the top policeman of all – Sir Charles – was flexible enough to meet these new demands. It was common knowledge that Sir Charles was in almost daily conflict with Home Secretary Matthews and there were many calls for the resignation of both men, not just in the papers but at a number of well-attended public meetings. Naturally, Sir Charles ignored the popular clamour. Resign? Why should he? Having thought that, he then put himself in a position where resignation became inevitable.

He wrote a pompous article for *Murray's Magazine* – a model of indiscretion. *The Gazette* said of it: 'There is some curious reading in Sir Charles Warren's paper on Sir Charles Warren, in *Murray's Magazine*:

The Commissioner starts off with the statement that London has for many years past 'been subject to the sinister influence of a mob stirred up into spasmodic action by restless demagogues. Their operations', he says, 'have exercised undue influence on the Government of the day, and year by year the metropolis of our empire has become more and more prone to dangerous panics, which, if permitted to increase in intensity, must certainly lead to disastrous consequences. If the citizens could only keep their heads cool and support the police in the legitimate execution of their duty there is nothing to be dreaded from the most powerful combination of the mob, but all peace and order will be imperilled if the citizens continue intermittently to join the mob in embarrassing those who are responsible for the security of the metropolis. It is still more to be regretted', continues Sir C. Warren, 'that ex-ministers, while in Opposition, have not hesitated to embarrass those in power by smiling on the insurgent mob. If we search history during the present century, we shall find that down to the year 1886 the mob or rabble exercised a decided influence over the destinies of London. In the spring of that year it overleaped all bounds, and London was subject to three days' reign of abject terror, pitiful and ridiculous, which only terminated because the mob was so completely astonished and taken aback at its own success that it was not prepared to continue its depredations.'

THE CLEARING OF TRAFALGAR-SQUARE
Passing to the events of last year, he says:- 'The mob, grown quiet since the previous spring, and they, thinking the police would now have no spirit to resist them, commenced proceedings which, but for vigorous measures,

ANOTHER MISS.

KEEPER MATTHEWS.—"P'RAPS IF YOU WAS TO SHOOT A LITTLE STRAIGHTER, SIR——"
   SIR CHARLES.—"DON'T TALK TO ME; IT'S THE WIND, AND THE GUN'S WRONG, AND IT'S ALL YOUR FAULT
—YOU'RE ALWAYS GETTING IN THE WAY."

might have resulted in the ruin of London. Before it was quite too late, however, a portion of the public saw the danger ahead, and rapidly rallied to the support of the police, and the clearing of Trafalgar-square was successfully accomplished without loss of life or destruction of property. Thus almost for the first time during this century the mob failed in its ascendency over London, and in coercing the Government, but it would be puerile to ignore the fact that there will be again efforts made to remove the destinies of the metropolis out of the hands of the people into those of the mob. Gradually peace has been restored, and security prevailing during the summer of 1888, signs were not wanting that another attack on the police was at hand. But this time it was to be of a more insidious character, being directed not so much against the individual police constables as against the police administration, and if successful it would effectually cripple the power of the executive to keep peace and order on the approaching Lord Mayor's Day. Fortunately, however, a note of alarm has been sounded in time, and citizens are beginning to rally round the side of law and order.

'It has been said that the police operations in Trafalgar-square were but military operations; it should be pointed out, however, that while the tactics were highly commended, the strategy was admired not only by experts at the clubs, but by the Social Democrats themselves; and there is a most interesting letter on the subject by Mr Morris in one of the democratic newspapers.'

WHY THE DETECTIVES DON'T DETECT

Sir Charles then gives an historical account of the London police, and goes on to explain why his detectives don't detect. He says :- 'The genius of the English race does not lend itself to elaborate detective operations similar to those practised on the Continent,' but he claims that 'Englishmen possess pre-eminently qualities which are essential to good detective work, such as dogged pertinacity in watching, thoroughness of purpose, and absence of imagination and downright sterling honesty.' In further comparing the French and English systems, he congratulates our Continental friends on the fact that 'the press does not venture to discuss their operations, to embarrass and hinder their inquiries, or to publish their results; though on the other hand, there is a distinct and serious loss to the community, police included, from the absence of a free press.'

POLICEMEN OR SOLDIERS?

Finally, Sir Charles repeats some not very candid criticisms which he has already made on our recent articles, and denies that he has 'militarised' the force. He says: 'It is quite untrue that there has been an attempt to make soldiers of the police, but there are certain attributes and qualifications which have been aimed at which pertain also to the soldier, sailor, postman, railway guard, or, in fact, to any citizen who joins an organised

82

service' and that 'it is also quite incorrect that a large number of reserve or discharged soldiers have been recently added to the police force'. Furthermore, we read that 'There can be very little doubt that the outcry against the police as a military force, so far as it is not instigated for special political or sinister purposes, is due to the Englishman who poses as a censor of public bodies possessing, as a rule, but one idea at a time. And he imagines that all his fellow-countrymen must be endowed exactly as himself . . .'

W. T. Stead, the Englishman in question, printed a biting retort to Sir Charles:

He is haunted by that great fiction. The vision of that vast predatory mob which established this bogus reign of terror in London is constantly before

IS DETECTION A FAILURE ?

In the interests of the Gutter Gazette and of the Criminal Classes, the Sensational Interviewer dogs the Detective's footsteps, and throws the strong light of publicity on his work. Under these circumstances, it is not surprising that Detection should prove a failure.

Was there just too much publicity?

THE TEMPTER.

SPIRIT OF ANARCHY. "*What! No work! Come and enlist with me,—I'll find work for you!!*"

his eyes . . . Poor Sir CHARLES! He is ridden by a nightmare, he sees the million-headed mob trampling onwards towards rapine, and no one else will realise its existence but himself. The cold sweat stands on his brow as he notes the composure with which we are all going about in our daily rounds, and so, forgetting all the reserve that is due to his position, he descends into the market-place, and cries aloud, 'The mob is upon you citizens! Support me, or you will be lost!'

And the citizens will not support him. On the contrary, they are laughing at him consumedly. They know that the so-called 'mob' is a phantom of Sir CHARLES's distempered imagination, and they will make short work of Sir CHARLES himself if he will not drop his absurd posturings as the Saviour of Society and stick to his business as a constable. There is no 'mob' in London in the sense in which Sir CHARLES uses the term. There are plenty of roughs and there are plenty of thieves. But they are such a handful compared with the honest folk, that we never even pay them the compliment of being frightened of them.

In his article Sir Charles had looked forward to the coming Lord Mayor's Procession, little dreaming that it would be marred and sullied, but not by the mob and not by the organised Reds and their unemployed cohorts. It was the Ripper once more. Jack chose that extra-special day to stage his most hideous ritual of all. It was butchery beyond belief.

Opposite: The spectre that haunted Warren.

THE · PENNY
ILLUSTRATED · PAPER
AND · ILLUSTRATED TIMES

No. 1488.—Vol. 55.

November 17, 1888.

REGISTERED AT THE GENERAL POST-OFFICE AS A NEWSPAPER.

London : Printed and Published at the Office, 10, Milford-lane, Strand, in the Parish of St. Clement Danes, in the County of Middlesex, by Thomas Fox, 10, Milford-lane, Strand, aforesaid.

THE MILLER-COURT MURDER, WHITECHAPEL: SITE OF MARY KELLY'S LODGINGS.

Thought that cause
there were not police
around Led cartidge
hurriedly etc

10
The Pinnacle of Horror

The axles were greased; the harness burnished with saddle-soap; the gilded coachwork polished to perfection. On the morning of 9 November 1888 the Lord Mayor's coach stood ready for the Procession down to St Paul's. Only a handful of people knew that a short distance away, Mary Kelly lay carved to pieces by the Ripper. All the other victims had been left on display, in the open, but Mary had been unwise enough to invite the man into her single room. And there, free from interruption, with all the time he wanted, the Ripper had indulged himself as never before. *Police News* reported:

> The victim was another of the unfortunate class, who occupied a miserably-furnished room in a court off Dorset-street, a narrow thoroughfare out of Commercial-street . . . Such a shocking state of things was there as has probably never been equalled in the annals of crime. The throat had been cut right across with a knife, nearly severing the head from the body. The abdomen had been ripped partially open, and both of the breasts had been cut from the body. The left arm, like the head, hung to the body by the skin only. The nose had been cut off, the forehead skinned, and the thighs, down to the feet, stripped of the flesh. The abdomen had been slashed with a knife across and downwards, and the liver and entrails wrenched away. The entrails and other portions of the frame were missing, but the liver, &c., it is said, were found placed between the feet of this poor victim. The flesh from the thighs and legs, together with the breasts and nose, had been placed by the murderer on the table, and one of the hands of the dead woman had been pushed into her stomach.

Newsboys shrieked out the first tidings of horror just as Lord Mayor Whitehead came within yards of the cathedral. The gilt splendour became overshadowed by the black news from the east. What would Sir Charles do now? Only a few knew that Warren was now powerless, that the night before he had tendered his resignation and it had promptly been accepted. His outburst in *Murray's Magazine* had proved too much. The Home Secretary had told Sir Charles that he had no right to

POLICE *THE ILLUSTRATED* NEWS

LAW COURTS AND WEEKLY RECORD

No. 1,292.   SATURDAY, NOVEMBER 17, 1888.   Price One Penny.

THE SEVENTH HORRIBLE MURDER BY THE MONSTER OF THE EAST-END.

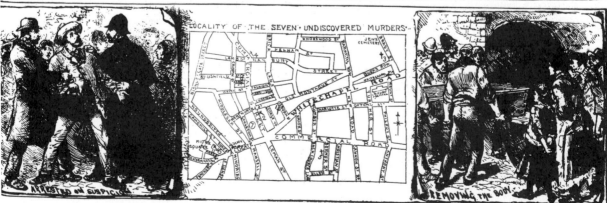

The most hideous butchery of all.

THE ILLUSTRATED POLICE NEWS

LAW COURTS AND WEEKLY RECORD

No. 1,295.   SATURDAY, DECEMBER 8, 1888.   Price One Penny.

EAST END HORRORS. WHEN WILL THEY CEASE?

THE WHITECHAPEL MURDERER'S RECORD.

FIRST MURDER — VICTIM — OSBORN STREET

SECOND MURDER — VICTIMS — GEORGE YARD

THIRD MURDER — VICTIM — BUCK'S ROW

FOURTH MURDER — VICTIM — HANBURY STREET

FIFTH MURDER — VICTIM — BERNER

SIXTH MURDER — VICTIM — MITRE SQUARE

Opening The Door To Admit Death!
MILLERS COURT, DORSET ST.

MURDER OF A BOY AT HAVANT

ARREST OF the BOY HUSBAND

A TERRIBLE CASE OF THROAT CUTTING NEAR CREWE.

publish any of his private views without permission. Sir Charles found such a restriction intolerable. It was obvious that the war of personalities between the two men had reached its peak. In went the resignation, and out went the Commissioner of Police.

By now, the interest in the Whitechapel murders was international. From America came a report that Jack the Ripper murders were taking place there. *Police News* reported: 'The people of Birmingham, in America, are very much exercised over a series of mysterious murders

MATTHEWS & WARREN.
"KNOCKABOUT" ARTISTES

An ignominious exit!

which have taken place in that neighbourhood. They are similar in character to the Whitechapel atrocities. The victims selected are negroes. There have been four of these tragedies within the last three weeks. No motive for the crime is apparent, and in each case the body of the victim has been horribly mutilated.'

Another *Police News* story involved 'A WHITECHAPEL CRIME IN AUSTRIA'. Its text read: 'A horrible double murder recalling in some of its revolting details the Whitechapel mysteries, is reported from ... Moravia. The bodies of two young girls, aged respectively seventeen and nineteen, were found a few days ago in the Forest of Leskau, frightfully mutilated. A gamekeeper named Schinzel lived there, with his two

90

AT LAST.

Warren's critics hailed his downfall.

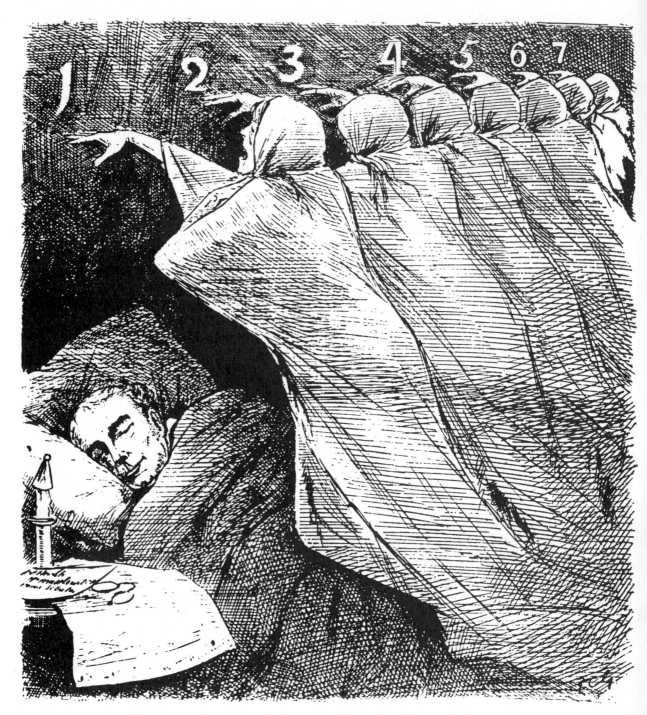

The Press dubbed Matthews 'helpless, heedless, useless'.

EXTREMES MEET.

Sir Edmund. "MY DEAR WARREN, YOU DID TOO MUCH!" Sir Charles. "AND YOU, MY DEAR HENDERSON, DID TOO LITTLE!!"
Mr. Punch (*sotto voce*). "H'M!—SORRY FOR THE *NEW MAN!!*"

And in came Monro.

daughters . . . his daughters were remarkably well brought up . . . the two girls . . . were both of them renowned for their beauty . . . the gamekeeper's daughters were seen in the Leskau Forest in company of two strangers but they never returned home, and for four days nothing was heard of them. On the fourth day a peasant discovered their bodies in the forest. The elder sister was shot through the temple and her two breasts were cut off. The younger sister was shot in the breast and neck, while a wooden stave pierced the lower part of the body, running into the ground.'

In London, the deep revulsion roused by the Kelly murder did little to curb the exhibitionists who drew a thrill out of posing as the killer and it

JACK THE KISSER.

A CRANK WHO ROAMS AT LARGE IN ST. LOUIS, MO., STOPPING MEMBERS OF THE FAIR SEX
ON THE STREET AND KISSING THEM BY FORCE.

JACK, THE KISSER.

[SUBJECT OF ILLUSTRATION.]

The extended currency given to the revolting exploits of "Jack, the Ripper" has stirred up all the cranks in the country, and St. Louis is not without her quota of them. They all seem to bid for notoriety, and the antics of some of these unbalanced people are decidedly funny. The latest to come to the front is "Jack, the Kisser," as he chooses to call himself. Osculation, under favorable circumstances, is greatly enjoyed by ladies; but the sensation of being suddenly grabbed by a stalwart individual, held firmly and kissed passionately is, to say the least, startling to sensitive and modest maidens. Yet hardly a night passes but one or more ladies are accosted and kissed by "Jack, the Kisser."

The new crank that has made his appearance within the last two weeks in St. Louis has been devoting his energies to the locality reaching from the Visitation Convent on Cass avenue up to Garrison avenue and the streets running north and south for a few blocks between these points.

Like all the other cranks that have sprung up since English "Jack" thrilled the world with his exploits, the "Kisser" has, as he claims, a mission to fulfill.

Several ladies along Cass avenue have, in their possession cards forced upon them by the individual who styles himself "Jack the Kisser." The card is crudely printed and bears the following inscription:

COMPLIMENTS OF

JACK THE KISSER.

Any lady who has been kissed three times by Jack and retains this card is entitled to membership in the Grand Army of the Redeemed. Jack's kiss purifies but never defiles. His mission is divine, and his kiss devoid of sensuality.

[Over.]

The reverse side of the card contains two verses of gushing poetry, fervently inscribed to the female sex.

did nothing to stop the flood of Ripper missives. *Police News* reported that:

> With the latest Whitechapel horror the silly practice of sending postcards signed 'Jack the Ripper' through the post has been renewed. Almost every day has brought a fresh batch into the hands of the police. People who receive them, instead of putting them behind the fire and forgetting all about them, consider it their business to take them to the nearest police-station and demand protection, believing that they are to be the objects of a visit. One would scarcely imagine that there were people in these days so easily frightened. We saw a young woman the other day who had received a postcard saying that 'Jack the Ripper' was coming to live in Birmingham and would call on her at a given date, and she was so alarmed that she implored the police to allow her to remain in the cells for a few days and nights. Of course the police could not grant her request, and though the date of the promised visit has passed we have not heard of any tragedy in the town. But private individuals are not the only people who receive attention from the nondescript. A prominent undertaker in the town the other day received a postcard, signed in the usual way and written in large black letters, asking him to send six coffins to *The Daily Mail* office by Saturday, and adding 'I will provide the corpses. The editor and his satellites are come for.'

In addition to the scrawlers, there grew an increase in the number of tellers of tall tales. *Police News* records the following:

> Mr Matthew Packer, the fruiterer who sold some grapes to a man in company with the murdered woman just before the Berner-street murder, has made the following extraordinary statement:- 'On Tuesday evening two men came to my house and bought 12 shillings worth of rabbits of me. They then asked me if I could give an exact description of the man to whom I sold the grapes and who was supposed to have committed the Berner-street and Mitre-square murders, as they were convinced they knew him and where to find him. In reply to some questions one of the men then said, "Well I am sorry to say that I firmly believe it is my own cousin. He is an Englishman by birth, but some time ago he went to America, stayed there a few years, and then came back to London about seven or eight months ago. On his return he came to see me, and his first words were, 'Well boss, how are you?' He asked me to have some walks out with him, and I did round Commercial-street and Whitechapel. I found that he was very much altered on his return, for he was thorough harem-scarem. We met a lot of Whitechapel women, and when we passed them he used to say to me, 'Do you see those? How do you think we used to serve them where I came from? Why, we used to cut their throats and rip them up. I could rip one of them up and get her inside out in no time.' He said, 'We Jack Rippers kill lots of women over there. You will hear of some of it being done over here soon, for

I am going to turn a London Jack Ripper.'" The man added "I did not take much notice then of what he said, as he had had a drop of drink, and I thought it was only his swagger and bounce of what he had been doing in America at some place which he mentioned, but I forget the name; but when I heard of the first woman being murdered and stabbed all over I then began to be very uneasy, and to wonder if he was really carrying out his threats. I did not however, like to say anything about him, as he is my own cousin. Then, as one murder followed another, I felt that I could scarely rest. He is a perfect monster towards women, especially when he has had a drop of drink. But, in addition to what he said to me about those murders in America and what was going to be done here, I feel certain it is him, because of the way those Jack Ripper letters which have appeared in the papers begin. They all begin 'Dear Boss' and that is just the way he begins his letters. He calls everybody 'Boss' when he speaks to them. I did not want to say anything about him if I could help it, so I wrote to him, but he did not answer my letter. Since this last murder I have felt that I could not remain silent any longer, for at least something ought to be done to put him under restraint." '

Packer states he feels sure the men are speaking the truth, as they seemed very much concerned and hardly knew what to do in the matter. He knows where to find the men. One is employed at some ironworks and the other at the West India Docks, and the man they allude to lives somewhere in the neighbourhood of Whitechapel.

The statement was investigated by the police. A reporter was courteously received on Thursday by Detective-Inspector M'Williams, who said there was no foundation in fact for it, and he believed that nothing would come of it.

Nothing, in fact, came of any of the many statements made to the police. House-to-house enquiries yielded nothing of great value; not one firm piece of evidence that could be tied in with any suspect came into the hands of the police. And by the end of the month some were convinced that the Kelly murder had sent the killer well over the brink into total madness, perhaps even suicide.

11

The Doldrums of December

December opened with a sense of emptiness. Many suspects had been taken in for questioning but not one of them was worth holding. The police were bewildered and weary. The killer stayed dormant, invisible, unfathomable. It became a time for stock-taking, with every manner of theory being re-examined.

From Russia came a theory first published in the paper *Novosti*. This was summarised in many English papers, amongst them *The Daily Chronicle*:

> *The Novosti*, in an article on the Whitechapel murders, expresses the belief that the perpetrator of these dreadful crimes is a Russian named Nicolai Vassilyeff, of whose past career it gives the following details. Vassilyeff, who was born at Tiraspol in 1847, was a student at the Odessa University, and having become a fanatical anarchist, he migrated to Paris in the 'seventies, where he shortly afterwards became insane, and was placed under restraint. Before being lodged in an asylum, however, Vassilyeff, whose mania appears to have been that fallen women could only atone for their sins and obtain redemption by being killed, murdered several unfortunates in Paris under conditions somewhat similar to those of the Whitechapel crimes; and on his arrest, his insanity having being proved, he was placed in a criminal lunatic asylum. This happened sixteen years ago, and Vassilyeff, or the mad Russian, as he was called, remained in the Paris asylum until shortly before the first Whitechapel outrage, when he was dismissed as cured. He is then said to have proceeded to London, where for some time he lived with the lower class of his fellow-countrymen. After the first Whitechapel murder, however, Vassilyeff was lost sight of, and the Russian residents in London believed that their insane countryman is no other that the murderer.

The Russian slant was obviously in complete conflict with another favourite theory of the day which had been aired in full in *The Gazette*. Its text ran:

> Allow me to suggest the solution of the London mysteries lies in the fact

that you have a Malay 'running a-muck' amongst a certain section of the community there. First let us consider the Malay nature as described by authorities:- 'The Malay race are extremely vindictive, treacherous and ferocious, implacable in their revenge, and on the slightest provocation, or imaginary insult, will commit murder. When bent on revenge they scarcely ever fail of wreaking their vengeance. Many shocking murders have been committed by Malays to gratify their thirst for revenge, which nothing but blood will satisfy, though at the certain loss of their own lives . . . Some parts of the bodies are missing. Why? Because this fiend has possessed himself of and preserved some, as the Indian warrior did the scalps of his victims. They have taken the place of his stolen savings, an equivalent for what he has lost . . .'

The conclusion was obvious; search for a Malay who is a ship's butcher, then check the dates of his arrivals and departures at the docks. If they fit, there's your man.

Much more to the point seemed to be the belief that Jack was actually seen, at very close quarters, by a lucky prostitute. Her name was Annie Farmer. After meeting a client, she downed far too much hot rum and became drunk. *Police News* reports:

The couple went to the common lodging-house, at No 19, Georges-street, and engaged a double bedroom . . . Nothing more was heard of them until about half-past nine (a.m.) when the man was heard to run downstairs, and presently the woman was heard following him and screaming out that he had tried to murder her. As soon as he reached the street the man set off at a smart run, and a number of men, attracted by the woman's screaming, went in pursuit of him. Strange to say, however, although the streets were thronged with people, no one ventured to stop the fugitive; and after a chase of three or four hundred yards he completely disappeared, and has not since been heard of. The inmates of the lodging house, seeing that the woman Farmer was bleeding from a wound in the throat, took her back to bed and sent for the police and a doctor. The first medical man to arrive was Dr Phillips, police surgeon, who soon announced that the wound in the throat was little more that superficial. An ambulance was sent for, and, as soon as the wound had been properly dressed, the woman was conveyed to Commercial-street police-station for examination. The woman was covered up, and it could not be seen whether the police were conveying a live person or a corpse. This, of course, added to the popular excitements, and strengthened the belief that another horrible murder and mutilation had been committed. Commercial-street was, in consequence, completely blocked, and the police had great difficulty in reaching their destination.

On arriving at the police-station Farmer was placed in a warm, comfortable room and interrogated. She was, however, in such a condition that neither a coherent narrative nor a satisfactory description of her assailant

POLICE *THE ILLUSTRATED* NEWS

LAW COURTS AND WEEKLY RECORD

No. 1,294.   **SATURDAY, DECEMBER 1, 1888.**   Price One Penny.

THE WHITECHAPEL MONSTER AGAIN SEEN SEEKING ANOTHER VICTIM: OUTRAGES AT THE EAST END.

Annie Farmer's 'near miss'.

could be obtained. It was not until the evening that the woman had sufficiently recovered to answer questions with anything like clearness, and the description which she ultimately gave of the attempt on her life and the appearance of the would-be murderer was somewhat confusing. It seems certain, however, that the man was not a stranger to Farmer, and that she had known him as a casual acquaintance for about twelve months. This, together with the evidence of some of the men who pursued the fugitive, has furnished the police with a clue which, it is hoped they will follow to a successful issue. The description of Farmer's assailant, as circulated by the police is as follows:-

'Wanted, for attempted murder, on the 21st inst., a man, aged thirty-six years, height five feet six inches, complexion dark, no whiskers, dark moustache. Dress: Black jacket, vest, and trousers, round black felt hat, respectable appearance; can be identified.'

The public read a great deal into the Annie Farmer encounter; the police entertained a very different view: to them it looked like a simple dispute between a dissatisfied client and a greedy harlot. Despite this, the Farmer affair was to form the basis of a vigorous Ripper-hunt in June the following year.

Later in 1888, in the last week of December, eyes were drawn away from London. From Bradford came the report of a gruesome murder headlined as; 'WORSE THAN THE WORST OF THE EAST-END CRIMES.' *The Gazette* carried a full report, part of which read: 'A boy aged eight years, named John Gill, was found by the police dead in a stable in Thorncliffe-road, Bradford . . . The body was even more shockingly mutilated than at first reported. Both arms and legs had been roughly chopped off. There were two stabs in the left chest. The heart had been torn out entirely, and was placed near the throat. Both boots had been taken off the feet, and pressed into the cavity in the abdomen, while the lower parts of the body were practically cut away. The police theory is that the crime is the act of drunken lads whose imagination had been inflamed by the accounts of the Whitechapel tragedies, and that they attempted in emulation, their worst features. The legs and arms were tied to the body when it was found, and the whole of the remains were wrapped in a coarse covering, making it look like a long oblong parcel.'

On the last day of the month *The Gazette* printed an item which now focused attention on New York:

Inspector Andrews, of Scotland-yard, has arrived in New York from Montreal. It is generally believed that he has received orders from England to commence his search in this city for the Whitechapel murderer. Mr

Andrews is reported to have said that there are half a dozen English detectives, two clerks, and one inspector employed in America in the same chase. Ten days ago Andrews brought hither from England Roland Gideon Israel Barnet, charged with helping wreck the Central Bank, Toronto, and since his arrival he has received orders which will keep him in America for some time. The supposed inaction of the Whitechapel murderer for a considerable period and the fact that a man suspected of knowing a good deal about this series of crimes left England for this side of the Atlantic three weeks ago, has, says the *Telegraph* correspondent, produced the impression that Jack the Ripper is in that country.

Five days before this column appeared, one of the contributing journalists to *The Pall Mall Gazette* paid a visit to Scotland Yard. There he wrote out an amazing statement, claiming that he knew the identity of the Ripper – two days earlier that very journalist had been accused of being the Ripper himself. And on the first day of the month he had contributed an extraordinary article to *The Gazette*, an article which ended by advancing a unique explanation for the murders – they were part of a black magic ritual. The article bore the by-line, 'By One Who Thinks He Knows'. It was written by Roslyn D'Onston – a man who certainly *did* know. A man who wrote with authority. The Ripper incarnate!

12
New Year; Old Fears

By the end of 1888 the police had discarded the idea that the Ripper had claimed at least eight victims; five only were chalked up to him. The press and public, however, remained mesmerised by the grander total, and waited for the inevitable next event.

Were they waiting in vain? Had the killer deserted the chilly Whitechapel streets for warmer, exotic sites? At one point, the press seemed to think so. On 18 February 1889 *The Gazette* made the following disclosure:

It would seem from the intelligence published this morning that 'Jack the Ripper' has transferred himself from the Old World to the New, and is practising his horrible crimes with as much impunity in the Far West as he did in the East of London. Some time ago it was reported that some unknown criminal had perpetrated several murders of the well-known Whitechapel type upon the outcast women in Jamaica. It will be seen from the paragraph which we quote from *The New York Sun*, that a similar outbreak of crime has occurred in Nicaragua.

The suggestion is obvious. When the Whitechapel murders were in progress a correspondent in Manchester sent to us an ingenious theory of the murders. He suggested that the murders and mutilations were in all probability performed by a ship's cook, who possibly enough was a Malay on one of the streamers plying to and from the port of London.

The last Whitechapel murder was committed on Lord Mayor's Day, November 9, since which time there have been no similar murders in the East of London.

We now learn that at the beginning of January similar atrocities were taking place in Nicaragua, and that about the end of December equally barbarous mutilations are reported from Jamaica.

It would be interesting to know whether any steamer left the Thames after the 9th of November, and after calling at Jamaica in December proceeded to Central America. If such a steamer exists there seems a strong probability that the murderer will be found among her crew – at any rate, the clue is one which might well be followed up by our detectives.

103

The New York Sun's text read:

[Managua, Jan. 24th] Either 'Jack the Ripper' of Whitechapel has emigrated from the scene of his ghastly murders or he has found one or more imitators in this part of Central America. The people have been greatly aroused by six of the most atrocious murders ever committed within the limits of this city. The murderer or murderers have vanished as quickly as 'Jack the Ripper', and no traces have been left for identification. All of the victims were women, and of the character of those who met their fate at the hands of the London murderer. Like those women of Whitechapel, they were women who had sunk to the lowest degradation of their calling. They have been found murdered just as mysteriously, and the evidences point to almost identical methods. Two were found butchered out of all recognition. Even their faces were horribly slashed, and in the cases of all the others their persons were frightfully disfigured. There is no doubt that a sharp instrument violently but dexterously used was the weapon that sent the poor creatures out of the world. Like 'Jack the Ripper's' victims, they have been found in out-of-the-way places, three of them in the suburbs of the town and the others in dark alleys and corners. Two of the victims were in the last stage of shabbiness and besottedness. In fact in almost every detail the crimes and the characteristics are identical with the Whitechapel horrors. All of the murders occurred in less than ten days, and as yet the perpetrator or perpetrators have not been apprehended. Every effort is being made to bring him or them to justice. The authorities have been stimulated in their efforts by the statement, which seems to be generally accepted, that 'Jack the Ripper' must have emigrated to Central America and selected this city for his temporary abode.

This imagined respite lasted only until 18 July. Then the London edition of *The New York Herald* proclaimed:

Jack the Ripper is back. He has returned from his supposed wanderings and resumed his hideous work. All the details of yesterday morning's crime as they came to light throughout the day leave no doubt in anybody's mind that the work was done by the same hand which has decorated Whitechapel with a string of atrocities unparalleled in history.

  All the murders have been audacious. The murderer has in each case taken chances which would have frightened any ordinary assassin from his purpose. But yesterday's murder beats them all in this respect. The police were in front of him, behind him, and all around him. There were three constables at least on watch within hearing of his victim's shriek, had his first blow failed. There was a lighted bedroom just above him, in which two people were going to bed . . . The woman was found lying diagonally across the narrow four-foot side-walk on the left-hand side of Castle-alley as you go in from Whitechapel-road . . . As the woman lay there it became evident

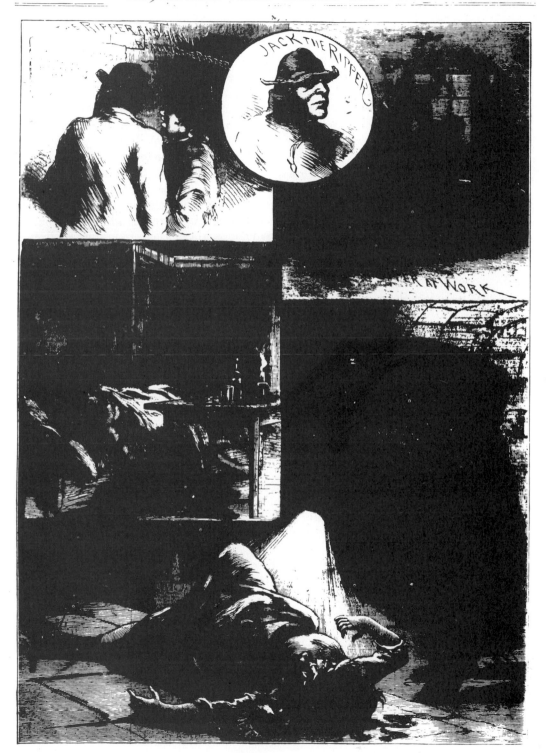

JACK THE RIPPER'S, TERRIBLE WORK.

SOME OF THE LATEST INCIDENTS CONNECTED WITH THE AWFUL CRIMES COMMITTED BY THE
MYSTERIOUS ASSASSIN, WHO IS BAFFLING THE LONDON POLICE.

The American view.

the 'Jack the Ripper' had departed slightly from his previous methods. She had been struck from behind like all the previous ones. But his method hitherto has been to stop the victim's mouth with his right hand, and with one heavy sweep draw the razor-like knife across the throat, severing the neck half through.

It was clearly evident yesterday . . . the the knife had been plunged into the left side of the neck and drawn backwards towards the back of the neck and the operator . . . When she was taken to the mortuary and closely examined the discovery was made that only the bluntness of the knife had prevented her from being as horribly dismembered as all the other victims . . . A blunt knife in 'Jack the Ripper's' hands is a strange discovery. All the other deaths and the subsequent mutilation had been done with a blade with the edge of a razor . . . The police stand as before, not knowing which way to turn. There is no doubt that they have done, and are doing, all in their power. Chief-Commissioner Monro and Colonel Monsell were on the spot as soon after the murder as the telegraph and cabs could bring them.

This murder of Alice McKenzie led to an incredible Ripper hunt organised by *The New York Herald* which at the time resurrected one of the anti-Jewish theories that had circulated in the previous year. As *The New York Herald* said:

It will be remembered that in November last it was suggested that the murderer came from one of the Continental ports aboard a meat boat, and, after perpetrating the crime, returned by the same vessel. The idea was in a manner ridiculed at the time. The police have now reasons to believe that the ridiculed suggestions of the murderer being a foreign Jew butcher had some foundation, and have issued instructions to the detective department accordingly.

It has been noticed that the crimes have invariably been committed about one a.m. on a Thursday or Friday morning. This led them to grow suspicious of these particular boats which arrive on Tuesdays and Thursdays and Wednesdays and Fridays and return the following day to their respective ports. The butchers employed aboard these boats land for the night intervening between their arrival and departure, and usually stay in the neighbourhood of Whitechapel. In view of these circumstances, it is reasonably contended that what is easier than for one of the Jew butchers, who it is known have a secret hatred of Christians, and for some reason have vowed revenge against a certain class of the East-end females, to land; get in company with his victim about the time of the closing of the public-houses; effect his hideous intentions; and retire a stranger to his lodgings at one o'clock in the morning. Blood on his clothes would not be regarded with suspicion when his avocation is explained; the knife used, which is known to be a pattern peculiar to butchers, would be a matter of no concern; and furthermore, the clean cuts inflicted on the victims are peculiar to the Jew's mode of killing cattle; and the doctor's testimony proves that the murderer has a knowledge of anatomy which, they stated, was acquired by the sheep butchers.

The authorities have ordered the East-end and Thames Police to inspect all cattle boats, and obtain from the visiting cattle-men an account of themselves on the 17th inst.

Seventy-seven years later the Jewish slaughterman idea formed the basis of a theory advanced by Robin O'Dell, yet in Victoria's time no investigation turned up a Jewish *shochet* (as they were called) who fitted the picture. No one was ever charged with the murder of McKenzie so, although differing in technique, the popular mind saw it as the Ripper's handiwork. Once again, two months later, another quite dissimilar murder was held to be the Ripper's.

The New York Herald (London edition) said on 11 September 1889:

London in general, and Whitechapel in particular, were thrown into a feverish state of excitement yesterday morning by the news that 'Jack the Ripper' had murdered and mutilated his ninth victim. Both the murder and mutilation were reported to be, and indeed proved to be, more horrible than in any one of the eight cases preceding . . . The mutilated body of 'Jack the Ripper's' latest victim, if such it is, was discovered about half-past five o'clock yesterday morning beneath a railway arch on the south side of Pinchin-street which runs eastward from Backchurch-lane, a narrow thoroughfare connecting Commercial-road with Cable-street . . .

The discovery was made by Officer Pennett . . . The remains were lying face downward. The head and legs had been removed and the sight was so grotesque and horrible that the constable was some seconds in making out what it really was. The horrible mass was partly covered by a blood-stained chemise, much disarranged . . . Scotland Yard was early astir . . . Chief Commissioner Monro and Colonel Monsell, Chief Constable, went all over the ground, and visited the mortuary. Identification will, in fact, be difficult if not impossible.

This latest murder stirred up the psychics once more, and *The New York Herald* devoted an ironic column to them, saying:

The occult experimentalists among them deceive only that portion of the public who wish to be deceived, and when people wish to be deceived they greet with utmost hostility any attempt to enlighten them. The good old British public, however, knows quite will that the seer and the clairvoyant and the mind-reader are still without any basis of recognised scientific facts or established physical principles to stand upon, and views them warily, very much as a trout of experience looks upon a bent worm which he knows has no business to be hanging there in the water.

It is into this class that the dreamers fall. They are private, not

professional dreamers, and between pride in their unhealthy way of
sleeping, ingenuity of imagination, and the wish which is the father to the
thought, manage to direct their telescopes of unconscious cerebration in
the particular, domestic or public, which is likely to make their narration of
it most interesting. They are entirely conscientious about it, and the
dreams about 'Jack the Ripper' which have been published in the newspapers would make a good-sized volume. In dreams he has been seen,
watched, followed along streets, followed to his house, followed to his
room, and dwelt with most intimately. The rooms and the descriptions of
Jack differ a little bit. In fact every new dream means a new situation, and
a new 'Jack the Ripper'. This simply arises from the fact, however, that the
dreamers had not read the same accounts, and eaten the same food before
starting on the dream hunt. It has been observed that a baked-apples-and-
cream 'Jack the Ripper' is usually much better dressed, and occupies a
better position socially than a welsh-rabbit 'Jack the Ripper', the latter
being the most ghoulish known to the extra-visual observers.

There is no doubt that the dreams take place, and that the dreamers
believe them. Mr T. Ross Scott, for instance, of Edinburgh, says he has
seen 'Jack the Ripper' three times while dreaming. Two of the dreams
occurred in July in Burntisland. The man seemed to him to be a ship's
surgeon, and seemed to be standing in a small dispensary. He could not
note the details because the ship's surgeon on both occasions so transfixed
Mr T. Ross Scott with his eye that he was glad to go out of the dispensary
and come back to Burntisland. Mr Scott, upon reading the published
version of a London thought-reader, was amazed to discover that they had
seen the same man, everything being similar in the two figures except the
colour of the moustache, which, of course, the figure could have dyed at a
trifling expense in the interim. The thought-reader was also gratified to
discover that a lady had seen the same figure in one of her dreams, though
the figure had left the dispensary, doubtless because it was Sunday, and
gone to evening service at a church, which was certainly a most natural
thing to do for a man who had such a large amount of repentance to
accomplish. Mr Scott's account of his last dream, which took place last
Tuesday morning, the morning of the finding of the last body, is both
typical and interesting. He says:-

'Retired to bed at half-past one this morning, but for a long while lay
quite awake. The last thing I remember was looking at my watch, the
hands of which pointed to five minutes to three. I then fell asleep.
Gradually buildings seemed to rise on every side, and I appeared to be
walking along a somewhat broad street, the features of which, however, I
was unable to see distinctly owing to the darkness of the night. While
proceeding on my way I became conscious of the presence of some one, and,
glancing up, observed a tall dark figure rapidly approaching me. In his
right hand the stranger held a large carpet bag, which apparently he had
considerable difficulty in carrying. As he passed he turned his head

towards me, and I immediately recognised him as the "surgeon" of my two previous dreams! In vain I tried to reach him; he again had his eyes fixed on me; I was totally unable to move. Just then I awoke struggling violently and completely exhausted. The time by my watch was eleven minutes past five.'

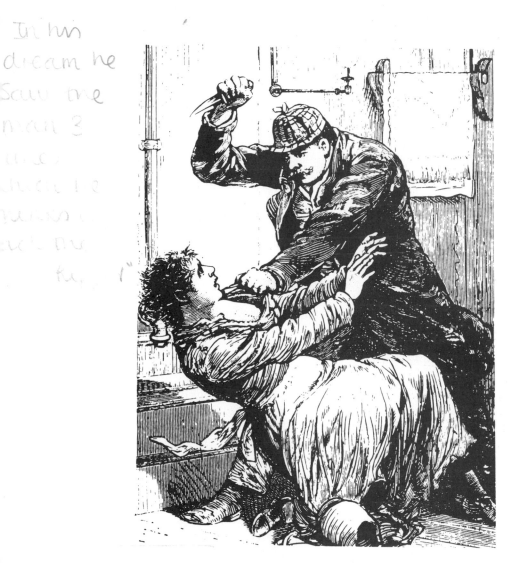

The Yanks were keen Ripper hunters: they
even located him in New Jersey.

Every bit as fanciful was the item run by *The National Police Gazette* in New York: 'Readers of the *Police Gazette* will perhaps remember that

IS THIS JACK THE RIPPER'S ACT?

GHASTLY ACTIONS ATTENDING THE FINDING OF THE REMAINS OF THE TWELFTH WHITECHAPEL VICTIM. SEPT. 10, 1899.

The *National Police Gazette* in New York claimed this to be
the Ripper's twelfth victim.

[handwritten: There was a note put onto the body & wouldn't rest until hed killed 15.]

when the first body was found a note was found pinned to the body which
stated that the perpetrator of the horrible crime would not rest content
until he had finished fifteen victims. The last is "Number 12" and three
yet remain.'

Despite such extravagant Yankee arithmetic, the London police still
listed the Ripper murders as five, dismissing McKenzie from the reckoning – she was someone else's victim, while the body under the arch was
most probably a morbid prank engineered by medical students.

The headless corpse proved to be the last 'Ripper' scare of 1889. There
were scores of false alarms to follow, but it was not until February 1891
that Jack's spectre was raised once more.

[handwritten: Feb. 1891 - it all appeared again.]

13
Fears Unquenched

The great Ripper scare of 1891 erupted on 13 February. Under a railway arch, off Royal Mint Street, police found Frances Coles slashed and ripped – still faintly alive. After her death they arrested James Thomas Sadler, a seaman who certainly knew Frances; in fact he had been with her the previous evening.

It was an evening he'd hardly forget – on leaving her he was jumped on, beaten up and robbed. In anger, he felt he'd been set up by Coles so he went back to her lodgings to confront her. But the lady wasn't there, she was out on the town once more. So Sadler wandered off into the night and became involved in a further fight, at the dock gates. He was found by the police drunk and bloody on a pavement only 500 yards from the murder site, but this was before the body was discovered. The police let him go and just minutes later they found Coles dying.

Sadler was arrested later that day and remanded in custody. There was public elation. *At last* the fiend had been trapped. Even the police felt they'd laid hold of a genuine killer – not a time-wasting drunk. But Sadler had staunch allies in his trades union. They paid for an investigation of their own. They unearthed evidence that supported Sadler's tales. He *had* been in a bloody fight outside the docks and at the time of the murder he was far too drunk to have carried out the killing and made good his escape.

It all ended as an anti-climax. Sadler was never brought to trial. although some among the police remained convinced he was guilty. Even so, nothing about Sadler made him an authentic candidate for the role of the Ripper. He was a man of ungovernable temper, loud-mouthed, more often drunk than sober – hardly the cunning, skilled butcher the police were really after.

From then on, it became certain that the Ripper proper had bowed out. Perhaps he was dead, or raving away in an asylum, or slinking around some foreign lanes. And that's how things stood until the first quarter of 1892.

Frederick Deeming.

Then, in April, the Ripper surfaced once again. Well, that's what the public thought. Yet this time there was no body left in the streets. There were bodies – but these were found laid under cemented floors. One was discovered in a house in Windsor, Australia, the others unearthed in a house at Rainhill, in England. The man behind these killings was con-man Frederick Deeming and at first there was nothing in his history to connect him with the Whitechapel killings.

A new view was taken of the man after his picture was published in the English papers. On seeing one of these, an East End girl visited *The Globe* offices and gave a startling interview. The paper's story read:

The theory that Deeming committed two or more of the Jack the Ripper murders in Whitechapel is now strengthened by an extraordinary state-ment which has reached us. It appears that a respectable girl, a dress-maker, resident in the East End, identified the portrait published in a weekly paper last Sunday as that of a man she knew by the name of Lawson in 1888. She states that she kept company with him in the autumn of that year, and in the evening of September 29th they went for a walk. Soon after 11 p.m. they parted at Portland-road Railway Station, and she returned home by train. On the following morning, shortly before one, the body of Elizabeth Stride was discovered with her throat cut . . . and an hour later a constable found the mutilated body of Mrs Eddowes in Mitre-square. The same afternoon the girl, who desires her name to be sup-pressed for the present, met the man Lawson by appointment, and went for a walk with him. His conversation was mostly of the murders, and she says he spoke with intimate knowledge of the details of the tragedies. During their walk, Lawson purchased a newspaper, in which it was stated that the murders were probably perpetrated soon after midnight. This passage he pointed out to her, exclaiming, 'Look at the time. I couldn't have committed them, could I?' This remark the girl declares she remem-bers distinctly, it being made quite voluntarily, but at that time it did not occur to her that the circumstances were suspicious. She says Lawson was on that afternoon greatly agitated, and betrayed an earnest desire to read the newspaper comments upon the crimes. A few days later, however, he disappeared, and they have not since met. Some little time afterwards she thought over the circumstances, and although she regarded them as extraordinary she refrained from communicating with the police. It was not until she saw the portrait of Deeming she resolved to make the statement, for she has no doubt whatever the man she knew as Lawson was the original of the published portrait. His general bearing coincided

Opposite: Sir Charles Warren, misplaced disciplinarian.

The Ripper learned to kill with Garibaldi –
did he change his sabre for a surgeon's knife?

directly with that of Deeming. He always made an ostentatious display of rings and spoke of his travels abroad.

Police News secured a copy of the full-length photograph the girl had referred to, and to the delight of the paper it turned out to be remarkably close to their artist's impression of a man seen with Mary Kelly on the day she died. Their artist had closely followed a description given by George Hutchinson, who had spoken of Kelly's companion as a man wearing a long, dark coat trimmed with astrakhan collar and cuffs with a dark-coloured jacket underneath this, worn over a light-coloured waist-coat. He wore buttoned boots and gaiters, sported a very thick gold watch-chain, and looked quite out of place in the grubby surroundings of Thrawl Street. He stood about five foot six tall; his complexion was pale; his hair dark; his slight moustache curled up at each end. He could possibly be Jewish; he was certainly respectable.

Here was a marvellous opportunity for *Police News*. It placed the original front-page drawing of 1888 alongside a drawing based on the vital photograph and made its visual point in the strongest possible way. Small wonder that many readers found the resemblance convincing enough for them to imagine that Jack was about to meet his end. Such illusions were strengthened by reports that Deeming himself had boasted to his warders that he was indeed the Ripper. Yet for all the furore it was meaningless. Deeming was a family murderer, pure and simple, not one to stalk the streets in search of strangers. And at the time of the murders, he was not even in the country. Believe it or not, though, for years his plaster death-mask was on display in Scotland Yard's Black Museum as the death-mask of Jack the Ripper.

The second pseudo-Ripper of 1892 was hanged in November. His name was Dr Thomas Neill Cream, convicted for poisoning prostitutes with strychnine capsules. So on the surface of things, there seems to be nothing to connect him with knife killings. The idea that he might be the Ripper arose out of two small events. The first was a threatening letter sent to Coroner Braxton Hicks. It read: 'The man that you have in your power, Dr Neill, is an innocent as you are. Knowing him by sight, I disguised myself like him, and made the acquaintance of the girls who had been poisoned. I gave them the pills to cure them of all their earthly miseries, and they died . . . If I were you I would release Dr T. Neill, or you might get into trouble . . . Beware all, I warn but once . . . Yours respectfully, Juan Pollen, alias Jack the Ripper.'

Such a letter was obviously worthless but it was the beginning of

113

speculation which then became reinforced by the claim that Cream's hangman had heard him shout out, 'I am Jack – ' just before the rope silenced him forever. *When cream was hanged he shoute*

[In recent years such trifles have been added to by journalist Donald Bell and handwriting examiner Derek Davis, in an attempt to show that Cream *was* the Ripper after all. But the whole cranky theory dies with a whimper when confronted by the fact that Cream was in Joliet Prison, in the United States, from November 1881 to July 1891.]

The final false Ripper-trail of 1892 involved a young woman named Emily Edith Smith. She allowed herself to be picked up by a perfect stranger in Cheapside who took her to tea in a coffee-house off Fenchurch Street, then induced her to take a bus-ride with him, a short ride that ended on the corner of Commercial Road. *Police News* reports:

She was unacquainted with the locality, and asked, 'Where are we now?' The man replied, 'This is Whitechapel.' The girl answered, 'Oh! Then this is where the girls were murdered.' 'Pshaw, not girls,' said the man deprecatingly, 'old women, you mean. They were better out of the way.' This was said in so quiet a manner that but little attention was paid to it by the girl . . .

At the corner of Commercial-road they entered a tramcar . . . and turned down Sutton-street. Here they visited a beerhouse . . . while passing down the Commercial-road he talked of the shops and the proprietors with the freedom of one who knew them very well, and before entering the tramcar pointed towards Leman-street, saying, 'That is where Jack the Ripper is best known.'

In the beerhouse . . . the girl for the first time closely observed her companion . . . He was tall and thin, looking like a consumptive, with high cheekbones, his face being pale. He stood over five foot nine, wore a hard bowler hat, had very dark hair, though his moustache, which was curled at either end, was of sandy tint. He had very peculiar eyebrows, meeting over the nose and the ends turning up towards the temples. She would have seemed to have taken particular notice of his eyes. These she described as odd and light, almost to squinting, one being a lightish brown and the other a bluey grey. He had a strange habit of blinking them but they sparkled and were piercing . . . His forehead seemed rather square, and although speaking English well, he struck her as being a foreigner . . . He walked with a military gait, spoke like an educated person . . .

Leaving the beerhouse in Sutton-street, the man and the girl walked towards the further end of it. The street, which is usually black and deserted, was, by reason of the fog, almost in darkness. One hundred yards down they passed under a railway arch, and turning to the right entered a long narrow passage, known as Station-place, which save for a few yards at the entrance, was enveloped in complete gloom. A new railway platform to the Whitechapel line of the Metropolitan Railway is in process of construction at one part of the passage, and a hoarding had been raised around a portion of the works. The girl said she would not venture further, and that she did not like the appearance of the place. The man urged that his offices were at the end of the lane. But the young woman would not advance with him. They were standing then in the gloom opposite an angle in the hoarding, which even had there been no fog, would have completely prevented any chance of their being seen. A street lamp, some few feet away, projecting from the opposite wall, shed but the faintest glimmer of light. 'Let us go on a bit further,' said the man. 'I will not,' replied the girl. 'Then I'll settle you now,' answered the man quietly. He caught the girl by the back of the collar of her dress and neck, and dragged her into the dark angle of the hoarding. They were face to face. He made to twist her round so that her back might be to him, and at that moment the girl saw a knife in his hand. The girl gave 'one big scream', and raising her right knee with all the power she could command dealt the man a violent blow in the lowest part of the abdomen. The man released his hold, and agonisingly exclaimed, 'Oh, my God!' then made a dive at the girl with the knife, but missing her, stumbled forward. The girl, screaming loudly, rushed into Sutton-street, where two women endeavoured to ascertain from her what had happened. The man was not seen again.

Such is the story which has been placed in the possession of the Scotland-yard authorities. It was submitted to Sir Edward Bradford the next day, and he at once placed it, with orders for full inquiry, in charge of Mr Donald Swanson, the chief inspector of the Criminal Investigation Department, who instructed Sergeant Bradshaw to accompany the girl over the route from Cheapside to the spot where the alleged murder was attempted. What gives the girl Smith's story the strongest interest is that her description of the man who accompanied her is almost word for word identical with that which the police authorities have always held to be the description of the appearance of the criminal for whose arrest they sought so eagerly two years ago . . . False

Was Miss Smith's account somewhat exaggerated? Was her assailant a Ripper-impersonator whose play-acting got out of hand? The matter was never satisfactorily resolved. In any case, it was not Jack's work – the killer was now inactive, incapable of further harm. The rituals were over.

Who was he then? Some felt that the Austrians had provided the answer. As *The Daily Graphic* reported:

A belief is prevalent in Vienna that the man Szemeredy, who was arrested on suspicion of being the author of the recent murders and robberies in that city, but who committed suicide while being interrogated by a police officer, is identical with the perpetrator of the mysterious Whitechapel murders. In regard to Szemeredy's antecedents it has been ascertained that he twice deserted from the Austrian army and escaped to Buenos Ayres, where charges of robbery and murder were preferred against him. In 1885 he was pronounced to be suffering from mental aberration, and was sent to a lunatic asylum, from which he was however discharged shortly afterwards as he was considered to be harmless.

No evidence has as yet been adduced to connect him with the White-chapel crimes, nor has it even been shown that he was in England. The president of the Vienna police, on being interviewed on the subject the other day said:- 'We know only one thing of Szemeredy – namely, that he was in Vienna in 1889 from August the 2nd to the 13th of that month, when he left, as he stated for America. You know that in Austria every stranger must on arrival fill up a police form, stating his name, profession, age &c., and here I show you two such forms filled up by Alios Szemeredy. He lived the first six days in Springer Gasse, and afterwards five days in Circus Gasse. In both forms he calls himself an "Amerikanischer Wun-darzt" (an American surgeon). His age is given as forty-nine, his con-fession Catholic, his condition single,and on the last form he says as to his destination, "Going to America." Whether he went to England instead to commit the crime detected in Whitechapel on September the 12th, I cannot say, but it is curious that on his later visit to Vienna in 1892 he described himself as "a sausage maker" .'

Szemeredy – who on earth has heard of such a suspect? His name is absent from the Ripperologists' reckonings. Yet, incredible as it may seem, Szemeredy was the subject of the first full-length book on Jack the Ripper, written by Carl Muusmann and called *Hvem var Jack the Ripper?*, published in Copenhagen, in 1908.

But if the Ripper *was* dead, strange scares still made news, like the item in *Police News* which ran: 'A bag marked, "Lot number one of J. Ripper", has been found at Hawthorne, a suburb of Melbourne. It contains the lower parts of a man's legs which had been evidently only recently severed from the body by a practised hand.' Another stupid prank by medical students? It carried all the hallmarks.

This was not the final hoax in the Ripper saga by any means – there were many more to come, but at the end of 1892 the police finally closed the Ripper files.

THE ILLUSTRATED POLICE NEWS

LAW·COURTS AND WEEKLY RECORD.

No. 1,467. | (REGISTERED FOR CIRCULATION IN THE UNITED KINGDOM AND ABROAD) | SATURDAY, MARCH 26, 1892. | Price One Penny.

THE APPALLING DISCOVERIES AT RAINHILL NEAR LIVERPOOL.

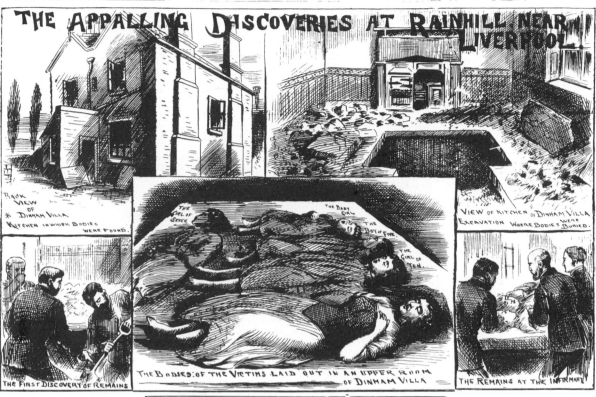

BACK VIEW OF DINHAM VILLA. KITCHEN IN WHICH BODIES WERE FOUND.

VIEW OF KITCHEN OF DINHAM VILLA EXCAVATION WHERE BODIES WERE BURIED.

THE FIRST DISCOVERY OF REMAINS

THE BODIES OF THE VICTIMS LAID OUT IN AN UPPER ROOM OF DINHAM VILLA

THE GIRL OF SEVEN. THE BABY GIRL. THE BOY OF FIVE. THE GIRL OF TEN.

THE REMAINS AT THE INFIRMARY

THE COMMERCIAL HOTEL

MATHER'S SHOP.

THE RAINHILL HORROR FROM SPECIAL SKETCHES.

MARIE. LILLA. BERT. MRS MARY DEEMING. MISS MATHER OF RAINHILL.

FREDERICK BAYLEY DEEMING, ALIAS LAWSON, OR WILL, CHARGED WITH MURDER IN AUSTRALIA AND SUSPECTED OF BEING THE AUTHOR OF THE RAINHILL TRAGEDIES.

STABLE YARD YARD BACK DOOR KITCHEN SINK SCULLERY PANTRY LOBBY PORCH DRAWING-ROOM DINING ROOM CARRIAGE DRIVE PLAN OF DINHAM VILLA LAWTON ROAD

DINHAM VILLA

THE ILLUSTRATED POLICE NEWS

LAW COURTS and WEEKLY RECORD.

No. 1,468. (REGISTERED FOR CIRCULATION IN THE UNITED KINGDOM AND ABROAD.)   SATURDAY, APRIL 2, 1892.   Price One Penny.

THE RAINHILL MURDERS: A REMARKABLE DREAM.

AUSTRALIAN-INCIDENTS, RAINHILL MURDER-MYSTERY

THE ILLUSTRATED POLICE NEWS

LAW·COURTS and WEEKLY RECORD.

No. 1,469   (REGISTERED FOR CIRCULATION IN THE UNITED KINGDOM AND ABROAD)   **SATURDAY, APRIL 9, 1892.**   Price One Penny.

INCIDENTS IN THE LIFE OF DEEMING THE RAINHILL MURDERER.

DEEMING AS A BIGAMIST.

DEEMING WANTED.

DIGGING HIS VICTIM'S GRAVE.

THE MURDER AT WINDSOR, Victoria. — THE CRUEL FATE OF A TRUSTING YOUNG WIFE.

HE FRAUD & PROCURES TWO MISTRESSES.

A BLACK MURDERED AT JOHANNESBURG.

DEFRAUDING A BANK AT DURBAN.

ROBBERY OF THE CAPE MAIL OF £5,000.

HIS HEALTH IS DRUNK WITH ENTHUSIASM.

HE SHAVES OFF HIS MOUSTACHE WITH A PIECE OF BOTTLE GLASS.

HE HAS SEVERAL FITS. FOUR STRONG MEN CAN SCARCELY HOLD HIM DOWN.

BANQUET AT THE COMMERCIAL HOTEL, RAINHILL.

HE PROPOSES TO MISS ROUNCESVELL AND IS ACCEPTED.

PLAYING AT DRAUGHTS WITH DETECTIVE ON BOARD 'THE BALLAARAT.'

HE IS KEPT IN IRONS ALL NIGHT AND CANNOT SLEEP.

ATTEMPT TO LYNCH PRISONER AT YORK STATION, WESTN AUSTRALIA.

POLICE NEWS
THE ILLUSTRATED
LAW COURTS AND WEEKLY RECORD

No. 1,293. SATURDAY, NOVEMBER 24, 1888. Price One Penny.

PORTRAIT SKETCHES OF SUPPOSED WHITECHAPEL MONSTER AND INCIDENTS IN THE CASE.

ATTEMPTED MURDER AT PECKHAM.

FATAL FIGHT AT NOTTING-HILL.

THROWING OUT BOILING WATER

SCENE AT AN IRISH EVICTION

Was Hutchinson right?

POLICE NEWS
THE ILLUSTRATED
LAW COURTS and WEEKLY RECORD.

No. 1,470. | SATURDAY, APRIL 16, 1892. | Price One Penny.

IS DEEMING "JACK-THE-RIPPER"?

THIS SKETCH APPEARED IN THE ILLUSTRATED POLICE NEWS SHORTLY AFTER THE WHITECHAPEL MURDERS IN 1888

THE DREADFUL ORDEAL THROUGH WHICH HE IS PASSING IS BREAKING DOWN HIS HEALTH.

DEEMING'S SLEEP IS FITFUL HE STARTS NERVOUSLY AT THE LEAST SOUND AND DEMANDS ITS MEANING

HUTCHINSON'S DESCRIPTION OF THE MAN SEEN ENTER THE HOUSE WITH THE VICTIM KELLY. THE DORSET ST. MURDER.

JACK-THE-RIPPER FROM VARIOUS DESCRIPTIONS GIVEN OUR SPECIAL ARTIST BY THE VICTIMS' FRIENDS.

DEEMING. FROM A RECENT PHOTO

DEEMING'S BRAVADO IN THE DOCK

IS SOON CHANGED TO DESPAIR WHEN IN HIS PRISON CELL!

THE TRIPLE MURDER AT BELFAST

24 HILLMAN STREET WHERE TRAGEDY OCCURRED

AFTER MURDERING HIS TWO CHILDREN SPILLER FINISHES HIS WIFE WITH A HAMMER

MRS MONTAGU CONVICTED OF THE MANSLAUGHTER OF HER LITTLE DAUGHTER 3 YEARS OLD AT COLORAINE

THE PRISONER ALLAN SPILLER

THE TRIPLE MURDER AT BELFAST

DISCOVERY OF THE BODIES

Was the dressmaker right?

THE ILLUSTRATED POLICE NEWS

Law Courts and Weekly Record.

No. 1,471. REGISTERED FOR CIRCULATION IN THE UNITED KINGDOM AND ABROAD.   SATURDAY, APRIL 23, 1892.   Price One Penny.

THE RAINHILL MONSTER,
AND HOW HE DID HIS AWFUL WORK.

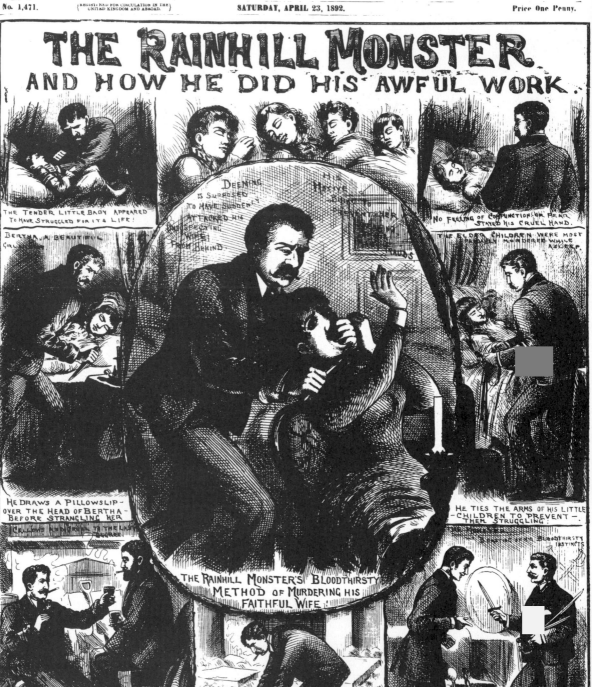

THE TENDER LITTLE BABY APPEARED TO HAVE STRUGGLED FOR ITS LIFE!

No FEELING OF COMPUNCTION OR FEAR STAYED HIS CRUEL HAND.

BERTHA A BEAUTIFUL GIRL

THE ELDER CHILDREN WERE MOST PROBABLY MURDERED WHILE ASLEEP

DEEMING IS SUPPOSED TO HAVE SUDDENLY ATTACKED HIS UNSUSPECTING WIFE FROM BEHIND

HE DRAWS A PILLOWSLIP OVER THE HEAD OF BERTHA BEFORE STRANGLING HER

HE TIES THE ARMS OF HIS LITTLE CHILDREN TO PREVENT THEIR STRUGGLING

THE RAINHILL MONSTER'S BLOODTHIRSTY METHOD OF MURDERING HIS FAITHFUL WIFE

THE ASSASSIN PLAYS THE PART OF A BOON COMPANION AFTER BURYING HIS VICTIMS.

THE RAINHILL MONSTER CEMENTING THE GRAVE OF HIS BUTCHERED FAMILY

DEEMING AND HIS COLLECTION OF AFRICAN ARMS.

THE ILLUSTRATED POLICE NEWS

LAW · COURTS and WEEKLY RECORD.

No. 1.472. {REGISTERED FOR CIRCULATION IN THE UNITED KINGDOM AND ABROAD.}   SATURDAY, APRIL 30, 1892.   Price One Penny.

THE·APPALLING·DISASTER·AT·HAMPSTEAD·HEATH·STATION

HAMPSTEAD MORTUARY.

WHERE INQUEST WILL BE HELD.

HORRIBLE DEATH OF A LAD

WAY OUT

STAIRCASE AT HAMPSTEAD HEATH STAT.
WHERE DISASTER OCCURRED.

MIRACULOUS RESCUE OF A BOY 6 YEARS OF AGE

DEEMING'S BITTER REFLECTIONS IN JAIL

BIGAMY

LUST

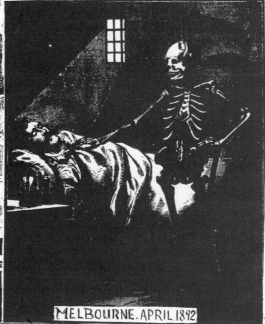

MELBOURNE. APRIL 1892

CONCEALMENT

ICE

THE ILLUSTRATED POLICE NEWS

LAW COURTS AND WEEKLY RECORD.

No. 1,473. [REGISTERED FOR CIRCULATION IN THE UNITED KINGDOM AND ABROAD]   SATURDAY, MAY 7, 1892.   Price One Penny

THE SHOCKING OUTRAGE IN PARIS BY ANARCHISTS.

THE ANARCHISTS AT WORK — PLACING THE BOMB IN POSITION — SENTENCED TO PENAL SERVITUDE FOR LIFE — FINDING M. VÉRY — ENTREZ L'HOTEL — AFTER THE OUTRAGE.

ANARCHISTS AT BOW-STREET

INSPECTOR M'LYNCKY — MR. W. J. RAMSAY, Printer — THE PRISONER CHARLES WILFRID MOWBRAY — MRS VAUGHAN, Magistrate — THE PRISONER DAVID JOHN NICOLLS — THOMAS CANTRELL — SERGEANT USHER.

THE ALLEGED OUTRAGE ON THE LONDON & BRIGHTON R'Y.

THE RAINHILL & MELBOURNE MURDERS — SOME FURTHER ILLUSTRATIONS

MISS M. S. PRICE — THE VILLA AT WINDSOR WHERE MRS WILLIAMS WAS MURDERED — THE PASSAGE — WHERE THE BODY WAS FOUND — ANOTHER VIEW — HON. PATRICK NUGENT.

THE ILLUSTRATED POLICE NEWS

LAW COURTS AND WEEKLY RECORD.

No. 1,476. | (REGISTERED FOR CIRCULATION IN THE UNITED KINGDOM AND ABROAD.) | SATURDAY, MAY 28, 1892. | Price One Penny.

EXECUTION OF DEEMING.

THE ILLUSTRATED POLICE NEWS

LAW COURTS AND WEEKLY RECORD.

No. 1,477. | (REGISTERED FOR CIRCULATION IN THE UNITED KINGDOM AND ABROAD) | SATURDAY, JUNE 4, 1892. | Price One Penny.

DEEMING'S DREAM THE NIGHT BEFORE HIS EXECUTION.

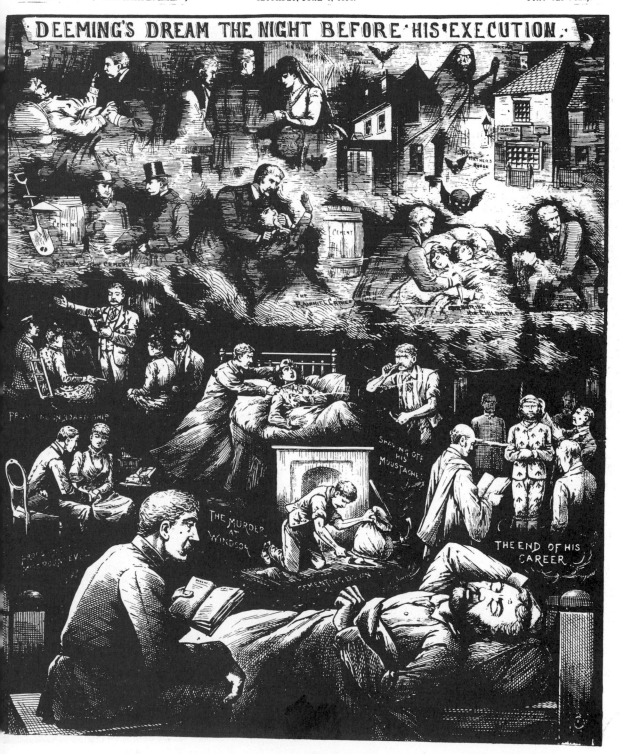

THE ILLUSTRATED POLICE NEWS

LAW COURTS AND WEEKLY RECORD.

No. 1,482. {REGISTERED FOR CIRCULATION IN THE UNITED KINGDOM AND ABROAD.}   SATURDAY, JULY 9, 1892.   Price One Penny.

TERRIBLE BALLOON DISASTER AT THE CRYSTAL PALACE

CAPTAIN DALE'S FAREWELL TO HIS WIFE

AN INSTANT BEFORE THE BALLOON BURST A WHITE CLOUD WAS SEEN AT THE TOP.

SHOWING BURSTING OF BALLOON.

SHOWING TOTAL COLLAPSE OF BALLOON.

DASHING TO DEATH.

REACHING THE EARTH

CAPTAIN DALE.

REMOVING THE REMAINS.

THE POISONING MYSTERIES.

LAURA SABATIN.

Mrs PHILLIPS.

THOMAS NEILL AT BOW STREET.

ELIZABETH MASTERS.

ELIZABETH MAY.

103 LAMBETH PALACE Rd WHERE NEILL LODGED.

BEFORE THE CORONER. NEILL'S AGITATION ON SEEING HIS BETROTHED

THE PRISONER HOOTED ON LEAVING THE CORONER'S COURT.

THE VESTRY HALL TOOTING.

THE ILLUSTRATED POLICE NEWS

LAW-COURTS and WEEKLY RECORD.

No. 1,483. {REGISTERED FOR CIRCULATION IN THE UNITED KINGDOM AND ABROAD.}   SATURDAY, JULY 16, 1892.   Price One Penny.

FATAL BALLOON ACCIDENT

A LADY LION-TAMER ATTACKED BY A LIONESS AT BRADFORD.

SHOCKING SUICIDE BY A LADY

THE Poisoning of Girls.

MR HAYES

COUNTESS RUSSELL

THE PRISONER NEILL

CHARLES HARVEY

THE SHOCKING MURDER AT BERMONDSEY

MRS LEA THE MURDERED WOMAN

A SON DISCOVERS THE BODY OF HIS MURDERED MOTHER

THE Poisoning of Girls.

G COWLEY

LITCHFIELD

INSPECTOR TONBRIDGE

LOUISA HARVEY

Shameful Treatment of a Horse

FIENDISH CRUELTY TO ANIMALS

Gross Cruelty to a Pet Lamb

Killing a Puppy

THE ILLUSTRATED
POLICE NEWS
LAW-COURTS AND WEEKLY RECORD.

EXCITING - ADVENTURE WITH A BURGLAR AT PIMLICO

BELGRAVE SQUARE WHERE BURGLARY OCCURRED.

WHERE BURGLAR ESCAPED.

THE STRUGGLE BELOW THE STAIRCASE

VOTE FOR
SNOGGLES
CHEAP
BEER & BACCA
PUBS
OPEN ALL DAY
ON SUNDAY

THE GENERAL ELECTION BY ONE WHO SAW IT

THE POISONING OF GIRLS: THE LAMBETH MYSTERY.

"HE GAVE ME SOME WHITE STUFF TO DRINK"

ALICE MARSH
ONE OF THE STAMFORD St VICTIMS
FROM A PHOTO

POLICE NEWS
THE ILLUSTRATED
LAW-COURTS AND WEEKLY RECORD.

No. 1,486.   {REGISTERED FOR CIRCULATION IN THE UNITED KINGDOM AND ABROAD.}   SATURDAY, AUGUST 6, 1892.   Price One Penny.

AN EXTRAORDINARY AND MOST REVOLTING TRAGEDY IN STIRLINGSHIRE.

THROWING LIGHT ON THE LAMBETH POISONING MYSTERY!

SERIOUS ACCIDENT TO THE HERNE-BAY AND CANTERBURY COACH

Police THE ILLUSTRATED News

LAW-COURTS AND WEEKLY RECORD.

No. 1,497. (REGISTERED FOR CIRCULATION IN THE UNITED KINGDOM AND ABROAD)   SATURDAY, OCTOBER 22, 1892.   Price One Penny.

THE GLASGOW HORROR

BLOOD STAINED ROOM

THE MURDERED WOMAN: FROM A PHOTOGRAPH

VIEW FROM MAXWELL DRIVE

WEST LODGE

X WHERE CRIME WAS COMMITTED

SUPPOSED RIPPER CRIME.

VIEW OF THE GARDEN SHEWING HOLES DUG FOR RECEPTION OF THE BODY

Wm. McEWAN THE MURDERER

+ BOX IN WHICH REMAINS WERE CARRIED FROM THE HOUSE BY WAY OF THE DOTTED LINE

McEWAN DISCOVERED BY GAMEKEEPER ENDEAVOURING TO CUT HIS THROAT

A CHAMPION BOXER SENT TO PRISON

A FEARFUL FATALITY IN A BEAR PIT

A SUSPECTED ANARCHIST

AT BOW ST.

SERGEANT WALSH

HE ONLY GAVE HIM A TAP

M. FRANCOIS, ALLEGED ACCOMPLICE OF THE LATE RAVACHOLS

NEILL AT THE OLD BAILEY

SKETCHES OF IMPORTANT PERSONS CONNECTED WITH THE CASE.

LAURA SABATINI

ELIZABETH MASTERS

ALICE MARSH, ONE OF THE VICTIMS.

THOMAS NEILL, IN THE DOCK.

MRS. PHILLIPS.

ELIZABETH MAY.

Jack was imagined to be everywhere.

THE ILLUSTRATED POLICE NEWS
LAW-COURTS and WEEKLY RECORD.

No. 1,498. REGISTERED FOR CIRCULATION IN THE UNITED KINGDOM AND ABROAD. SATURDAY, OCTOBER 29, 1892. Price One Penny.

THE GLASGOW HORROR.
LATER SKETCHES AND DETAILS.

McDOUGALL WHO DISCOV'D THE CRIME.

THE HEAD OF MARY ANDERSON AFTER IT WAS TAKEN FROM THE EARTH.

W'M McEWAN FROM A LATER SKETCH.

AXE AND SAW FOUND IN LUMBER ROOM SUPPOSED TO HAVE BEEN USED IN DISMEMBERING BODY.

THE HORRIBLE DISCOVERY IN THE GARDEN.

A PLAN OF WEST LODGE.

NORTH — GARDEN — EAST — WEST — PLAN OF HOUSE — WALL — ROOM — ROAD — WHERE MURDER TOOK PLACE.

THE HEAD FOUND.

THE LAMBETH POISONING CASE
NEILL'S CAREER.

NEILL AS A SCHOOLBOY.

NEILL FOLLOWING MATILDA CLOVER.

MARSH & SHRIVELL TAKING THE FATAL PILLS.

BUYING SPECTACLES.

HE GIVES 2 TO LOUISA HARRIS.

... THE CORONER.

THE NIGHT BEFORE THE VERDICT HE SLEPT WELL.

AT BOW STREET LAURA SABATINI HIS BETROTHED GIVING EVIDENCE.

AT THE OLD BAILEY SENTENCED TO DEATH!

FRIGHTFUL TRAGEDY AT OLDHAM

VICTIMS CORSET.

CARVING KNIFE FOUND.

CON AMBROO.

THE ACCUSED.

... WHERE THE ... DEED ...

DISCOVERY OF THE CRIME.

AWFUL MUTILATION CASE

MRS MELLOR THE MURDERED WOMAN FROM A PHOTO.

INTERIOR OF KITCHEN AS SEEN THROUGH THE WINDOW.

WHERE THE BODY WAS DISCOVERED.

DISCOVERING THE BODY.

THE ILLUSTRATED POLICE NEWS

LAW COURTS AND WEEKLY RECORD.

No. 1,499. (REGISTERED FOR CIRCULATION IN THE UNITED KINGDOM AND ABROAD) SATURDAY, NOVEMBER 5, 1892. Price One Penny.

THE JUST END OF A MONSTER OF INIQUITY.

CRIMES IN AMERICA

THE POOR GIRL DONWORTH WAS GIVEN SOMETHING OUT OF A BOTTLE BY A CROSS-EYED GENTLEMAN WITH SPECTACLES

AND HE LEFT HER TO DIE IN FRIGHTFUL AGONY IN THE STREET

HE MIXED HER SOME LEMONADE BUT SHE DIDN'T DRINK IT

HE WAS SEEN LEAVING THE HOUSE IN STAMFORD ST

NEILL OBTAINING POISON

LU HARVEY'S NARROW ESCAPE

THE DYING GIRL CLOVER CALLS FOR HER CHILD

HIS CEASELESS TONGUE BETRAYED HIM TO THE POLICE

IMPORTER

WANTED

THE WOMAN POISONER SEEKING HIS VICTIMS.
STAMFORD ST MURDERS

THE CONDEMNED MAN NEILL MENTALLY REVIEWS HIS AWFUL PAST

THE AWFUL TRAGEDY AT OLDHAM
FURTHER SKETCHES

MELLOR STOOD IN THE DOCK UNMOVED

TWO FILES, COAL SHOVEL & BLOOD STAINED CARVING KNIFE, FOUND ON THE PREMISES

MELLOR BEFORE THE CORONER

THE ARREST

OH MY POOR SISTER!

BACK OF HOUSE LOOKING FROM YARD DOOR

THE GLASGOW HORROR
FURTHER SKETCHES

McEWAN MEETING ELIZABETH O'CONNOR

THE VICTIM CAROUSING WITH HER MURDERER

THE GAMEKEEPERS WATCHING McEWAN

APPREHENSION OF McEWAN

POLICE NEWS

THE ILLUSTRATED

LAW-COURTS and WEEKLY RECORD.

No. 15;0.
SATURDAY, NOVEMBER 12, 1892.
Price One Penny.

ANOTHER DREADFUL TRAGEDY AT OLDHAM

MRS SMYTH. LIEUT LEADER. MRS. LEADER.

THE DIAMOND BROOCH SLANDER ACTION

MAJOR SMYTH

STUFFING PINS IN A BABY'S MOUTH

ANOTHER OLDHAM TRAGEDY.

MURDER AND SUICIDE.

NEILL RESPITED

THE JUDGE PASSING SENTENCE

NEILL READING HIS RESPITE.

ATTACKED BY BURGLARS BRIXTON.

HE SPRANG OUT OF BED AND SEIZED THEM

HE WENT THROWN DOWN THE STAIRS

THE TERRIBLE DISASTER TO THE SCOTCH EXPRESS NEAR THIRSK

PULLMAN SLEEPING CAR

THE WRECKED ENGINE

RESCUING THE DEAD & INJURED

SCENE OF ACCIDENT.

THE SIGNAL BOX

THE ILLUSTRATED POLICE NEWS

LAW—COURTS AND WEEKLY RECORD.

No. 1,501.   (REGISTERED FOR CIRCULATION IN THE UNITED KINGDOM AND ABROAD)   **SATURDAY, NOVEMBER 19, 1892.**   Price One Penny.

THE EXECUTION OF DR NEILL CREAM.

INTERIOR OF NEWGATE.

FLOGGING BLOCK FOR GORROTTERS

NEILL INFORMED THAT THE PLEA OF INSANITY WAS OF NO AVAIL

THE CONDEMNED CELL

BIRD-CAGE WALK, INTERIOR OF NEWGATE, WHERE MURDERERS ARE BURIED.

HIS LAST SLEEP

HIS LAST MEAL

THE BURIAL OF DR NEILL

NEILL'S GRAVE IN NEWGATE

DR NEILL'S LAST WALK ON EARTH

CLOSING SCENES IN THE CAREER OF A GREAT CRIMINAL.

THE JURY VIEWING THE BODY OF THE CRIMINAL.

THE ILLUSTRATED POLICE NEWS

LAW-COURTS and WEEKLY RECORD.

No. 1,502. {REGISTERED FOR CIRCULATION IN THE UNITED KINGDOM AND ABROAD.}   SATURDAY, NOVEMBER 26, 1892.   Price One Penny.

A MURDER TRAP BY THE THAMES FROM SKETCHES

THE MURDER TRAP. SKETCHED FROM A BOAT

THE ENTRANCE TO THAMES MURDER TRAP.

"YOU HAVE NOT PAID" HE GROWLED

TRAGIC END TO A LONG COURTSHIP.

DARING OUTRAGE AT LEWISHAM.

THE MURDER OF A GIRL AT BLACKBURN

THE RED HANDKERCHIEF TAKEN FROM THE CHILD'S MOUTH

DUCKWORTH, THE ACCUSED. SKETCHED AT THE INQUEST

THE BOOT FOUND TO FIT INTO FOOTPRINTS

ALICE BARNES THE MURDERED GIRL, FROM A PHOTO.

WHERE THE STRUGGLE TOOK PLACE

WHERE BODY WAS FOUND X

HOME OF ACCUSED

DR NEILLS DREAM THE NIGHT BEFORE HIS EXECUTION

Sir Melville Macnaghten – creator of false trails.

14

Raw Heat from the Sun

Find confusion and you find journalists. Repeatedly dubious newpaper copy has spawned false trails. The notorious Lees hoaxes of 1895 and 1931 and their ramifications are fully dealt with in my *Jack the Ripper: The Bloody Truth*. But *The Sun*'s 'scoop' of February 1894 has never yet been fully evaluated.

It began with a promising lead – a whisper that the Ripper was safely behind bars at Broadmoor Asylum. The investigation opened. Then, on 13 February, the first article appeared, proclaiming: 'We know the Christian name and surname of Jack the Ripper. We know his present habitation; our representatives have seen him, and we have in our possession a mass of declarations, documents and other proofs of his identity.'

In *The Sun*'s view, this man had killed nine times and further assaulted six women by stabbing them from behind. Their nominee '. . . was at liberty and close to Whitechapel during all that period when the murders were committed, and these murders immediately came to an end . . . from the moment he was safely under lock and key'.

No name was given but the paper gave its reasons for that, saying: 'At this moment our readers must be satisfied with less information than is at our disposal. Jack the Ripper has relatives; they are some of them in positions which would make them a target for natural curiosity . . .'

The man they were pointing at was, in fact, a mildly dangerous fetishist named Thomas Cutbush. Like 'Monster' Renwick Williams, Cutbush felt impelled to slash women's dresses from behind. His connection with the Ripper murders was nil.

One would have expected Scotland Yard to react to such articles with bored indifference, but it was otherwise. The then Commissioner of Police himself, Melville Macnaghten, took time off to write a lengthy, private rebuttal of *The Sun*'s claims. So why did he take the trouble?

The answer lies back in the black days of the Turf Frauds Scandal. The

139

public outcry at the time had never been forgotten and the bitter internal investigations within the police force had left its scars. Never again would the force be put in the position where it could be accused of covering up crimes committed by its officers or by anyone of importance. Yet by pointing to Thomas Cutbush, *The Sun* was actually indicting the nephew of the Superintendent Executive of the Metropolitan Police. Now, Macnaghten knew that Cutbush was not a killer – the records proved that – so in his notes he named three suspects 'more likely . . . to be the killer'.

The men he named were 'M. J. Druitt, said to be a doctor [in fact he was a barrister] . . . whose body . . . was found in the Thames . . . Kosminski, a Polish Jew . . . removed to a lunatic asylum about March 1889 . . .' and 'Michael Ostrog, a Russian doctor and a convict, who was frequently detained in a lunatic asylum as a homicidal maniac'.

These notes of Macnaghten's have bedevilled and confused the issues ever since but they were well meant. They told the truth as he saw it, and they were on record in case rumours about Cutbush got out of hand. In that event the police would need them. And Macnaghten feared that they might.

True, at first, *The Sun* was unwilling to publish the name of their Broadmoor suspect, but how long would they hold to that position? Not long, Macnaghten felt. He had good reasons for his doubts, for he knew the paper's editor was under pressure to reveal all.

The editor involved was T. P. O'Connor, a gentleman who led a double life as newspaperman and Member of Parliament. He had the reputation of being able to be in two places at once. It was said of him, and in all seriousness, that he was seen on the Commons benches on a day when he was known in fact to be in Ireland, by the side of his dying father! He also had a more deserved reputation for toughness and a love of flamboyant sensations. Just how long could such a man be trusted?

O'Connor himself gave Macnaghten good reason to feel uneasy, for on 19 February TP signalled his intentions in his editorial. This significant piece, missed by all commentators, is now printed for the first time since 1894. It reads: 'THE DISCOVERY OF JACK THE RIPPER':

Slowly, but steadily, the public has come to the same conclusion as that to which we have been forced by months of investigation – that in the witless wretch who is at present in Broadmoor Lunatic Asylum we have traced the author of the Whitechapel murders. We are not surprised that our statement should at first have been received with a certain degree of incredulity. Theories with regard to the identity of the murderer have been presented to the public by the score; time has passed away, and the theory has been forgotten. In the first article, too, which we published on the subject, we had to be satisfied with giving nothing beyond the broad outlines of our information. The manner in which we came to publish the article throws some light on contemporary journalistic methods. We had this information for months in our office, for months representatives of the paper have been searching for witnesses, examining them, often hunting them only after weeks of patient labour. It was not our intention to have

T. P. O'Connor was supposedly seen in The House of Commons
when he was in Ireland.

published the story for some weeks to come; but on Monday night I was called out to the Lobby of the House of Commons by two of my staff, to tell me that a portion of our information was to be offered to two morning papers. I am glad to say, for the credit of journalism, that the *Morning* ——— (a Conservative contemporary) refused to have anything to do with a discovery the credit of which belonged to another office; in other quarters the taste and the honour were not so delicate as we had anticipated, and there was consequently nothing for it but to stop up all night, and bring out *The Sun* as a morning paper at five o'clock instead of an evening paper at the usual hour. Our staff - editorial, compositors, machine-men, and cart men – were summoned; we all stayed through the watches of the night in consultation and in preparing the matter for publication; and day had already broken before any of us were able to start for our homes. It will be understood under these circumstances how our story on the first day suffered from indefiniteness; we were simply marking time, and had to wait the opportunity of further consultation with our legal advisers before we could bring before the public the full materials at our command.

What reserve we had to make to defeat the arts of rivals, we were bound still further to increase by our sense of the public welfare and our desire to spare feeling. Many correspondents have written to us to demand that we should give the name of 'Jack the Ripper' to the public. We may have to do so in the end, but we shall do so unwillingly, for it is hard to make the innocent suffer for the guilty, and to expose the unhappy relatives – if such there still be – to the reprobation which will gather around his name. But we shall send to the police, when they ask for it, all the material at our disposal. The names which we had to veil under initials will be revealed to them. We have likewise the addresses, the occupations, all the particulars, with regard to all the persons who can either entirely reveal or throw considerable light on the mystery we claim to have solved. We understand that the attention of the highest police authorities has been called to our statements, and we confidently look forward to our story being subjected to the closest and most searching investigation. We believe that with others, as with us, facts will point irresistibly to the conclusion that the man we point out is undoubtedly the long-sought criminal.

It will after all be a relief to the public mind to feel that this inhuman – or, rather, non-human – monster is safe from all possibility of doing further harm. He has reached the stage when the decay of the mind has almost become complete, and probably the process of mental deterioration had already proceeded far enough to make him quite unconscious of his acts at the time when he committed the murders. From what we know of him – from the description given of him by our representative in the interview he had with him at Broadmoor – it is quite plain that mental derangement has produced an absolute eclipse of the moral nature. This man would commit a murder not only without remorse, but perhaps even without power of realising it a short time after he has committed it. It was thus possible for him to leave the scene of one of his crimes with but a partial recollection of what he had done. He would have neither terror nor remorse because he was destitute of mind and memory. In short, he would just feel after one of his crimes as might a tiger which had devoured a human being.

It is awful to think that human nature is capable of descending to these bestial depths; but in these things we must face the issue clearly and boldly; and if human beings of this kind exist – and they do – we must patiently analyse, study, dissect them until we come to the physiological basis of their abnormality. A complete study of this creature in his

Broadmoor cell ought to give science some clue to the intimacy of the connection between the loss of brain power and the loss of moral conscience. Probably all this awful and fiendish wickedness and cruelty will be traceable to some lesion of the brain – inherited from dead ancestors – and aggravated by the habits of the creature's own idle, dissolute, and worthless life. It is a great thing to have set the public mind at rest as to the possibility of a repetition of these crimes; but it is a much more important matter to have facilitated such a study of this monstrosity as will cast the light of science and complete knowledge along the black and sinister ways of crime, insanity, and homicidal instinct. In giving science the chance of thus adding to its knowledge, we claim to have done it a service which journalism has rarely equalled. Finally, the months we devoted to the investigation of the case, the pains with which we examined every particle of available evidence, the attempts – usually successful, sometimes defeated – to wring out the heart of the mystery – all these things will testify to the fact that we did not come before the public with our theory until we had thoroughly investigated and tried it by every means at our disposal.

Having digested this, with its hints of name-disclosures, Macnaghten, as a precaution in case of a rumpus, filed his statement at the Yard. And there it lay, potential ammunition for his underlings in the event of anyone raising a cry of 'cover-up'. Though marked 'Confidential', it was never meant to be a secret document – only the names were meant to be kept under wraps. Indeed, the document was carefully leaked to friendly outsiders, like Major Arthur Griffiths.

Fortunately, O'Connor played fair and no public connections were made between the Broadmoor inmate and the Metropolitan Police. But the vagueness and shortcomings of Macnaghten's exposition must raise important questions. Just how well-informed were the police? *Did* they have any firm ideas about the Ripper's identity?

Sir Robert Anderson – a lot to answer for.

15
A Choice of Villains?

Any answers to the queries raised by the Macnaghten papers must involve the outpourings of the centenary year. Almost every 'solution' now brought forward ultimately derives from police assertions made some time after the murders. Now, the men making those statements were mainly high-placed so their positions should have given them an unique chance to know the truth. Yet, strangely, they are at odds with each other. Why so?

Macnaghten, in his first pronouncements of 1894, gave equal prominence to three leading suspects: Druitt, Ostrog and Kosminski. Yet, with time, he came down in favour of Druitt. Even so his information on Druitt is tenuous and flawed, and his choice of the man rests on nothing stronger than a *belief*.

By contrast, Sir Robert Anderson pushed forward a deranged Jew as the killer. In his first presentation of this view, in an article in *Blackwood's Magazine* (March 1910) he said: 'The conclusion we came to was that he and his people were low-class Jews, for it is a remarkable fact that people of that class in the East End will not give up one of their number to Gentile justice, and the result proved that our diagnosis was right on every point.' He then repeated the charge in his autobiography. His confident words are worth remembering. He said: 'I am almost tempted to disclose the identity of the murderer. But no public benefit would result from such a course. I will merely add that the only person who ever saw the murderer unhesitatingly identified the suspect the instant he was confronted with him; but he refused to give evidence against him. In saying he was a Polish Jew I am merely stating a definitely ascertained fact.'

Who are we to believe – Macnaghten with his English barrister, or Anderson with his alien Jew? Of the two, Anderson makes the strongest claim by far but does he really have strength on his side, or is it arrant dogmatism? Sir Henry Smith of the City Police, for one, refused to accept Anderson's account, rightly pointing out that: 'Surely Sir Robert cannot believe that while the Jews, as he asserts, were entering into this conspiracy to defeat the ends of justice, there was no one among them with sufficient knowledge of the criminal law to warn them of the risks they were running.' He then went on to refer to *Stephen's Digest*, 'an absolutely reliable work on criminal law', saying: 'In murder cases accessories after the fact are liable to penal servitude for life; and thus the Jews in the East End, against whom Sir Robert Anderson made his reckless accusation, come under that category.'

Sir Henry was dead on target. It is absurd in the extreme to imagine that the police would have stood aside, thwarted and impotent, while a gaggle of conspirators protected a murderer. And not just any murderer, but the vilest one of all. It is simply past believing.

Was Anderson always so flighty with the truth? Not always, but often enough to have it remarked on. In the same article in *Blackwood's* he also claimed that he had written the articles for *The Times* on 'Parnellism and Crime' after gaining permission from his superior, James Monro. Upon reading this, Monro wrote a repudiation that was read to the Commons by the Home Secretary, Winston Churchill. It ended: 'No such authority was asked by Mr Anderson, and none was given to him by me . . . A long time afterwards, Mr Anderson informed me that he had written one or more of the articles, and I felt much annoyed.' At which the Irish Member Macveagh interjected: 'Then the statement of Sir Robert Anderson that he had official permission to write these articles is another edition of Anderson's Fairy Tales.' 'I don't think I could have expressed it better,' replied Churchill, and went on to speak of Anderson's '. . . gross boastfulness . . . and garrulous and inaccurate indiscretion of advancing years'.

Other police officers have had their own dissenting ideas. In 1903 Inspector Abberline said: 'You must understand that we have never believed all those stories about Jack the Ripper being dead, or that he was a lunatic or anything of that kind.' In fact, that year Fred Abberline himself quirkily named wife-poisoner Klosowski, alias Chapman, as the Ripper. With others, odd, furtive doctors feature – but all these preferences have to be discounted. The truth is that no one was caught in the act, and no overwhelming evidence was accumulated that would justify a trial. With nothing tangible to grapple with, the police had to fall back on the hopelessly inadequate store of knowledge of their time.

In 1888 there was only a meagre understanding of the complexities of the criminal mind. There were no archives dealing with serial-murderers driven by sexual lusts. There was but an elementary knowledge of the varieties and lures of sexual aberrations. Of necessity, the conclusions drawn reflected the shallow thinking and prejudices of the day – so the killer was a madman, most likely a foreign madman and probably not a Christian. As a consequence the three men on Macnaghten's list, the three main suspects, are docketed as insane. Anderson's Polish Jew is likewise a maniac. Our present-day state of knowledge tells us that such a view was far too simplistic.

We now know that the serial-murderer is often well able to live a life that is outwardly normal – even respectable. Such a man, in 1888, would never have been looked at twice, indeed if he had a valid reason for being out and about at night he would have been accepted as part of the scenery. The real Ripper counted on this. And he was right.

Unfortunately some centenary theorists remain shackled to the errors of the past. One hundred years of trekking the barren trails should have had a chastening effect but Anderson and Macnaghten still figure as blind leaders of the blind. Thus Macnaghten's tragic Druitt is the villain in the Martin Howells/Keith Skinner collaboration, *The Ripper Legacy*, while Martin Fido opts for another Macnaghten suspect, Kosminski, and identifies him as the Polish Jew indicted by Anderson. The two camps naturally can't agree, but does either of them merit more than some well-earned applause?

From my standpoint, the only way to judge these rival theories is to apply to them the same standards that I apply to my own work. Having done that, I find faulty and incomplete research in both cases. Add to that wayward reasoning, and we have good grounds for suspecting that the conclusions will be addled. And so they are.

The Ripper Legacy rightly rejects two spurious pieces of earlier Ripperologist lore. One is the conspiracy theory of Sickert and Knight, with its involvement of Sir William Gull and the Duke of Clarence. The other is the 'Mad Russian' theory based on the bogus 'Dr Dutton Diaries' and William Le Queux's inventions. Having done that, the joint authors then erect *their own* conspiracy theory involving the Duke of Clarence, and draw on the 'Dutton Diaries' to give the theory strength.

Their conspiracy is made to revolve around a predominantly homosexual society in Cambridge which came to be known as The Apostles and in the 1880's centred on Trinity College, the very place where Prince Albert Victor was sent to broaden his outlook. The authors establish, to *their* satisfaction, a series of suggestive links between Montague Druitt and several of the Apostles. No direct links are proven, though. It is a little different with Albert Victor, Duke of Clarence. He knew some of these Apostles quite well but there is nothing to show that he knew Druitt. The authors have convinced themselves that he did.

Officially Druitt drowned himself in the Thames, but this is far too tame for a conspiracy theory. He was *murdered*, state the authors, murdered by the privileged clique of homosexuals in order to protect themselves and those cherished by them – especially dear, dear Eddy, Duke of Clarence. Murdered, because they found out about Druitt's deadly drives. We are told that: 'For a time the welfare of a future King of England had been placed in their hands, with disastrous results. The discovery that Jack the Ripper was one of their number merely activated the machinery by which the real power in the land – the masters, servants and agents of obscure government departments – protects the *status quo*.'

This machinery, so it seems, was set in motion and Druitt was lured to his death at Chiswick. But why Chiswick? Well, that was the place where Apostle Henry Wilson, close friend of Prince Eddy, had his house, termed by him 'a chummery', a refuge where 'a succession of young men, chiefly from Cambridge, found an ideal substitute for the lonely and uncomfortable lodgings . . . and where other friends could always find youthful and cheeful company'. For Druitt, though, it was to be the place where all cheer ended. With stones in his pockets, he was carried out of the house and, covered by the dark night, dumped into the river.

The sole support for this startling scenario is that the body was found floating near Wilson's house. But this find was made on 31 December 1888, and the body had then been in the river for three to four weeks. Are we expected to believe that it had stayed put, in one spot, for all that time? And were the conspirators so stupid that they dumped their victim on their own watery doorstep?

What is so sad about this theory is that the authors have been taken in by a myth which is scarcely 30 years old. The involvement of the Duke of Clarence in the Ripper murders, in any role whatsoever, results from modern fantasies that were fertilised by earlier hoaxes. In my book *The Bloody Truth* I have shown how these fantasies evolved. They all stem back to the 1895 Ripper hoax concocted by journalists in Chicago. Regrettably, my book came too late to alert Howells and Skinner; by then they were publicly committed to their Royal involvement.

A CHOICE OF VILLAINS?

1888

The blameless Duke of Clarence (standing second from right) dragged in once more.

RUBBISH!!

Let me state as emphatically as possible that no diaries, newspaper columns, letters or books *prior* to 1960 have ever tied the Clarence name to the Ripper murders. As a matter of course, then, all present-day theories along those lines stand self-condemned.

In a similar fashion any theories drawing on the 'Dr Dutton Diaries' are invalid. In *The Bloody Truth* I demonstrate how and why these papers are sheer fiction. Yet Howells and Skinner, even though they suspect as much, drop their standards when they find a Dutton passage that helps their case. They quote from a statement alleged to have been made by Albert Bachert, one of the prime activists in the Whitechapel Vigilance Committee. In part this reads: 'I was given this information in confidence about March, 1889 . . . I was then asked if I would be sworn to secrecy . . . Foolishly, I agreed. It was then suggested to me that the Vigilance Committee and its patrols might be disbanded as the police were quite certain that the Ripper was dead . . . "It isn't necessary for you to know any more," I was told. "The man in question is dead. He was fished out of the Thames two months ago . . ."'

A statement like that obviously points to Montague Druitt, and if true would reveal an authentic police view of his suicide, a view reached significantly soon after the finding of his corpse. But the statement is worthless. It first appeared in print in 1959. It is without any proofs of ancestry and it is extracted from the same false memoirs that carry the stamp 'Dutton'.

The Ripper Legacy is further devalued by yet another hoax. The authors take some ten pages to mull over a strange story told by Edwin Woodhall. For them it is pregnant with meaning, even if muddled. What a pity they didn't realise that when it came to writing, ex-detective Woodhall acted as a thorough rogue. By the 1930s he had developed an appallingly bad memory but he cockily bluffed his way through page after page of his book on the Ripper. What he couldn't recall he invented. He even tampered with texts that lay in front of him. And among the stories he concocted was one involving the suicide of a weird Ripper suspect.

According to Woodhall, this man with a blackened face and white-painted eyes had terrorised women in Whitechapel. He was captured after a lengthy and fierce fight, taken to Scotland Yard for interrogation and met there by two highly placed officials. When left alone with these officials, he seized a heavy ebony ruler, knocked both of them out and made good his escape. Three weeks later, a paddleboat moored to

Waterloo Pier was moved. It displaced a corpse that had become jammed under a paddle-wheel. 'The black burnt cork and the white paint on the already decomposing features was hideously evident,' wrote Woodhall, who continued, 'Who he was, and where he came from, or anything at all about him, is . . . a complete mystery . . .'

Howells and Skinner seize on this story as full of clues to the cover-up that they are looking for. They ponder over the identity of the black-faced man and conclude that it was an insane medical student named John Sanders. Tortuously, they reason that the arrest and the events that followed form part of a pattern designed to draw attention away from Druitt. They conclude: 'Fortunately, however, a decoy had readily presented itself in the shape of John Sanders, alias White-eyes.'

Every conclusion drawn by them is wrong – hopelessly wrong. The black-face/white-eye saga is a pastiche of unrelated stories muddled together by Woodhall's confused and uncaring mind. He gave the imaginary events some sort of shape and threw in cheap melodrama to cater for a public that he knew had neither the time, energy nor inclination to check his story out.

Yes, there had been a body fished out of the Thames after being jammed between the paddle-wheels of a moored steamer, but it was the body of a *woman* and it was recovered on 8 October 1888, five weeks before the arrest of Blackface. As for Blackface, he was a real person but very different from the caricature presented by Woodhall. He fancied himself as an amateur detective. His blackened face was his own naive idea of a disguise – as a stoker perhaps. When first arrested, he claimed to be a doctor connected with St George's Hospital and the joint authors mention this. But they missed the vital sequel to this arrest. On Monday, 12 November *The Globe* reported: 'The police were apparently under the impression that they had 'Jack the Ripper', for they ordered the station to be cleared of all strangers when the man was brought in. To the dismay of the officers present the prisoner announced that he was a doctor connected with St George's Hospital, and gave the name of Holt and an address at Willesden. Mr Holt, after being detained for nearly three hours and a half, had his identity sufficiently established to enable him to proceed to his home.'

So there was no mystery surrounding the man. His name, address and place of work were confirmed in hours. There was no visit and fight at Scotland Yard, and no suicide. Those facts combine to give the death-blow to Woodhall's synthetic mystery. By using this and the other flawed material, Howells and Skinner have devalued their contribution. They meant well, but they leave Druitt as shadowy as ever.

Martin Fido tried another tack and went in search of the neglected candidate, Kosminski. Macnaghten's papers said that Kosminski was a Polish Jew resident in Whitechapel: 'He had a great hatred of women, especially of the prostitute class, and had strong homicidal tendencies: he was removed to a lunatic asylum about March 1889. There were many crimes connected with this man which made him a strong "suspect".'

With these clues in mind Martin Fido began a diligent search through the records of public asylums and work-house infirmaries. He failed to find a Kosminski held as early as March 1889 but he did find one admitted to Colney Hatch Asylum on 6 February 1891. This was 26-year-old Aaron Kosminski and he came from Whitechapel. Yet nothing in this man's records even hinted at a violent nature. There was no mention of crimes or strong homicidal tendencies. He was simply a poor wretch suffering from delusions, a sad figure impelled to search for bread in the gutters of the streets.

Fido had reluctantly to conclude: '. . . with eighteen months of harmless scavenging from the gutters from 1888 to 1890, Kosminski could not have been the Ripper.' So was his search abortive? Far from it, for along the way Fido had made notes on some other characters and now he began to see a link between them.

Basing his reasoning on the topography of the murders, he first took note of Nathan Kaminsky. Kaminsky was a Polish Jew who on 24 March 1888 began a six-week course of treatment for syphilis at the Whitechapel Workhouse Infirmary. After treatment finished he vanished from public records. In fact, nothing concrete is known about him from that moment on. Nevertheless, Fido creates a biography for him based on some very odd juxtapositions.

Four days after that first visit to the infirmary, Ada Wilson was attacked. We have already noticed this event and its lack of connection with the Ripper but Fido thinks differently, arguing that her assailant had features matching descriptions of clients later seen with Annie Chapman, Elizabeth Stride and Catherine Eddowes. On this basis he seems to visualise Kaminsky making his first murderous moves.

Using mental legerdemain, Fido then equates Kaminsky with Leather Apron, who '. . . throughout the summer . . . terrorised the streetwalkers within easy reach of his home'. He finally identifies Kaminsky as the young demented Polish Jew picked up on the Whitechapel streets at the beginning of December 1888 and sent on to Colney Hatch, under restraint. He was registered under the name David Cohen, proved too violent to be allowed to mix and died from 'exhaustion of mania' in October 1889.

Of Cohen's death Fido writes: '. . . thus, finally, Jack the Ripper succumbed almost as pathetic at the end as the victims of his frenzy'. He then goes on to say: 'Simple elimination of all other Jewish lunatics makes David Cohen Anderson's Polish Jew.'

If only it were so simple. Just weeks after Fido's book was launched *The Daily Telegraph* published some previously unknown jottings made by Chief Inspector Donald Swanson – comments written on the pages of Swanson's copy of Sir Robert Anderson's autobiography. His comments on Anderson's claim that the murderer had been identified by a man who refused to testify against him read: 'because the suspect was also a Jew and also because his evidence would convict the suspect, and witness would be the means of murderer being hanged which he did not wish to be left on his mind. And after this identification, which suspect knew, no other murder of this kind took place in London.'

On the endpaper of the book Swanson wrote a most remarkable observation. It reads: 'Continuing from page 138 after the suspect had been identified at the Seaside Home where he had been sent by us with difficulty in order to subject him to identification, and he knew he was identified. On suspect's return to his brother's house in Whitechapel he was watched by police (City CID) by day and night. In a very short time the suspect, with his hands tied behind his back, was sent to Stepney Workhouse and then to Colney Hatch and died shortly afterwards – Kosminsky was the suspect.'

Swanson puts no dates on record, but the Seaside Home he mentions was the Police Convalescent Home at Brighton which only opened in March 1890. By that time David Cohen was dead and buried. Apart from that, Cohen had no next of kin hence no 'brother's house' to return to. Martin Fido's Ripper-Cohen is patently not the same as Swanson's Ripper-Kosminski. Despite that, Fido has gone on record saying: 'I am quite convinced that he [Swanson] confirms my thesis that Aaron Kosminski who lived at "his brother's house" in Whitechapel was somehow confused with David Cohen, who probably committed the Whitechapel murders . . .'

The stark truth is somewhat different. The police testimony is in complete disarray and there is no legitimate way of reconciling the absurdities now revealed. I cannot accept that the police allowed anyone to flout the law, refuse to testify and then escape the consequences. Neither can I accept that the police needed to drag a reluctant suspect all the way from Whitechapel to Brighton simply to have him identified – the proposition is laughable.

The Swanson jottings, together with Anderson's and Macnaghten's writings, fully demonstrate that the uncertainties of 1888 became, with time, hardened into rigid convictions. Druitt, Ostrog and Kosminski are no more than the high points of those mounds of uncertainty. To find the real killer we have to spurn convention and delve elsewhere.

16
A Passion for Darkness

I once felt that we would never identify the killer yet finally I came to name D'Onston Stephenson as the only man who can be taken seriously as the Ripper. When I first reached that conclusion I knew that my research was far from complete. Still, even on that basis, I felt more than confident. I drew up profiles of every known suspect, even the zany ones. I posed the same questions in each case. He alone, of all the suspects, had the right profile, the opportunities, the motives, and the ideal cover. His background, his personality, his skills, his frame of mind, all fitted him for the fateful role. But has that original verdict of mine stood up to prolonged scrutiny? Has it needed to be revised – to be made more cautious, perhaps? The best answer to those queries is to assemble my new findings and draw up a fresh portrait of the man himself.

First we have to clear the ground. There is a conflict of dates in different sections of his autobiographical sketches. At one point he speaks of his first meeting with Bulwer Lytton, the writer who taught him all about 'Black Magic' and dates this encounter back to 1863. Yet in another sketch he says he'd known Lytton before venturing to Italy in 1860. How can we cope with such confusion? The sensible way is to gauge if the conflicts are serious enough to matter. We do this by looking at other autobiographies, lives of widely different characters. Having done so we realise that confused chronologies are rife: dates seem to transpose themselves readily, even in the keenest of minds. Sir Henry Wood, for example, was hopelessly confused when placing past events while author Frank Richards wrote of himself, 'He remembers verses by the thousands: master games of chess by the dozen. But his mind seems to jib at precise dates.'

One more question still needs to be asked. Does D'Onston benefit in any way from altering or adjusting any of his dates? Boasters and liars have often tried to gain credence by such calendar juggling, like the soldier who swore he'd seen the Angels of Mons. Private 10515 Cleaver of the First Cheshires actually signed an affidavit before a magistrate attesting to the visions at Mons. Unfortunately for him, his army records showed that he was still square-bashing in England on the vital days. Could D'Onston, then, be playing such a game? The answer is emphatically no. His confusion brings him no advantage – not the slightest.

Bulwer Lytton put 'magic'
in the wrong hands.

Taking his life from its start in April 1841, we find someone whose problems were all of his own making. His family was rich and generous enough to allow him to study where he chose. In his teens he took rooms in Munich and studied chemistry under the renowned Dr James Allan – the former right-hand assistant to Baron Liebig. Other medical studies were pursued in Paris and there he met the son of Lord Lytton. The meeting came like some sign from Heaven, for D'Onston was in awe of the light revealed by Lytton's book *Zanoni* – a novel based on the power of magic. Through the son he met the father, and began delving into the heady, murky world of the magicians – both White and Black.

Then, for a while, there were other distractions. Like countless other reckless, bright-eyed students, he was ensnared by the fire and fury of Garibaldi's rising and joined the redshirts in the mainland campaign of 1860, both fighting and patching up the wounded, along the bloody route to Salerno.

It was a victorious few months and then it was all over. The invigorating existence, the rough comradeship, was replaced by passive medical studies and infantile student carousings, an old routine which seemed empty and arid. Only magical studies allowed one to dream and gave promise of fresh excitements and revelations, so the books were bundled up and he set off for the west coast of Africa to view the wonders wrought by witch-doctors.

It was a foolhardy, vagabond existence, hardly likely to meet with family approval. When his funds sank too low, his family put him under pressure and he returned home, in 1863, to take up a safe, predictable and boring post with the Customs in Hull. It was a post he treated with contempt. 'Almost a sinecure,' he termed it. He even left the service for a whole year, then rejoined in 1866. His service records show that he persistently antagonised his superior officers, but in his own eyes he was naturally superior to all the manikins around him, whatever their rank.

By 1867 his father was not only a prominent manufacturer but the Collector of Hull Corporation Dues. His elder brother was a shipowner, partner in Rayner, Stephenson & Co., and Vice-Consul for Uruguay. Yet not even family influence could shield him from Nemesis.

In March 1868 he was charged with being absent from duty and called before a disciplinary board. Only one day was involved, but before that there had been other days and in front of the board was an admonition for D'Onston from the London Headquarters. It referred to the previous year and noted that he: '. . . causes at times much inconvenience to the Service by want of attention to his duties and by the irregularity of his attendance'.

At his hearing he called an outsider, Alex Fowler, who stated: 'I met Mr [D'Onston] Stephenson a little before 9 o'clock in the morning in consequence of a letter which I had received from a mutual friend, materially affecting Mr Stephenson. It was necessary that it should be immediately attended to that day, as the tenor of this letter seriously affected Mr Stephenson's prospects and character. From my knowledge of the facts of the case, I believe it would have been too late, had he deferred attending to the matter until the next day.'

Hull seemed willing to accept this defence but London HQ insisted that the nature of the private business had to be disclosed to the Collector at Hull. The Collector then reported: '... his absence was caused by information given him that certain matters prejudicial to his moral character had been communicated to the lady he is about to marry, and it was of great importance to his future welfare, that he should at once refute them'.

The report goes no further but we now know that a family crisis had hit the Stephensons. D'Onston had earlier been involved with Ada-Louise, a prostitute in Hull. Like George Gissing, he entertained the illusion that he could rescue such a lady, he would even marry her. But his family had other plans for him. The daughter of a local wealthy family, a girl already attracted to D'Onston, was the ideal partner – the woman of the streets quite unacceptable.

The family was able to enforce its will when D'Onston ran up large gambling debts, his father refusing to pay these off unless his son broke off all contact with the prostitute and agreed to marry the heiress. D'Onston gave in, though he did arrange to see Ada once a year; a typically Victorian, poignant tryst, on a lonely bridge at midnight.

Later, in July 1868, yet another crisis hit the Stephensons. D'Onston was shot in the right thigh by Thomas Piles, a fisherman and yawl-owner of Hull. One-and-a-quarter ounces of lead shot had to be cut out from the thigh by the coastguard surgeon, and D'Onston had to lie immobile for some three weeks before he could be returned to his home. In fact, he remained away from his Customs post for a total of 169 days.

The shooting was bound to have raised serious questions about D'Onston's reliability within the Customs Service. He described the shooting as a hunting accident but the man who shot him had a reputation as a *smuggler*. What was a Customs Officer doing in befriending such a man? Was the smuggler benefiting from inside knowledge of Customs plans? Was the wounding the result of a quarrel between knaves?

While his employers debated over his character faults, D'Onston tried to keep his promised tryst with Ada. On the agreed night, an old family servant wheeled him in a bath chair across the town to the deserted bridge. The girl never came. By then she was dead, yet D'Onston swore he'd seen her cross the bridge. He'd even heard the clink of the brass heels she favoured. This vivid hallucination marked a new phase in his personality change. When operating on his thigh, the surgeon would have made free with his injections of pain-killing morphia and the same drug would have been at D'Onston's daily disposal from then on as he recovered. In that year, as articles in *The Practitioner* show, doctors believed that there were no dangers involved in injecting morphia, even over long periods. Within two years they were to learn otherwise but by then D'Onston was a drug addict.

Whatever Hull Customs discovered about him is still unknown – the records are infuriatingly incomplete – but on his return to duty he was dismissed from the Service: 'Struck off the establishment' is the official wording. Shortly afterwards Robert D'Onston Stephenson ceased to exist. He changed his name to Roslyn D'Onston, left Hull for London and covered up all traces of his past life as a servant of the Crown.

Some family funds still came his way and he was able to travel around, ever searching for Grand Magic. As his writings show, he even took this gruelling search to India, investigating many a fakir. It was all in vain, though. Whenever he felt he'd touched the hem of real magic, it was always illusion or deception. Yet he was gullible enough to go on believing.

Years of his life still remain a mystery but everything points to a steady decline in his fortunes. It wasn't poverty, at first; he simply became more and more a loner, with his brain tormented by delusions of grandeur, fired by drugs and drink and his belief in the power of magic. One day he would make a breakthrough, his knowledge of the occult would change his status and astonish the sheep-like masses.

There is police evidence, though, that at one point realism overtook dreaming. D'Onston made a different bid for status – he was even prepared to discard his Bohemian ways and commit himself to a regular, responsible post. Ironically, it was a post serving, and controlled by, the police.

In July 1886 the secretaryship of the Metropolitan and City Police Orphanage fell vacant and was advertised. The salary was £200 a year but the successful candidate had to give security for the sum of £500. Among the candidates was Roslyn D'Onston. The man who remained convinced of his own intellectual superiority was not even short-listed. Had he reached that list he would have found himself face-to-face with Sir Charles Warren, who chaired the selection board. Had he been chosen, then the Whitechapel murders would never have happened: the post offered long-term stability and recognition; it also involved living over the orphanage at Wellesley House in Twickenham – far from the dark alleys and slum rooms and hideaways of the East End.

The post went to Arthur Kestin, a respectable managing clerk, the sort of man D'Onston would despise. D'Onston saw his rejection as a personal affront – he had no means of knowing that the post had attracted 372 other candidates. He put thoughts of conformity behind and resigned himself to the vagabond life, a life that led him downwards to the seamy pleasures of the East End gin palaces, and to rooms in malodorous Whitechapel.

Less than two years later his fantasies peaked and the killings began. We can never know the full story of those first, chilling moments of decision. We can only guess at the trigger factors that set off his plan of ritual murders. The burdens of a wasted life; the irrational leaps of a drug-stimulated mind; the perverse allure of the unknown and untried. All these factors may have combined to push him into his satanic experiment. And 'satanic' is the key word that allows us to open a door into the twisted mind of D'Onston and others like him.

Today we hear very little of Black Magic but in the latter part of the nineteenth century there was a strong interest shown in all branches of magic, an interest by no means confined to the semi-literate. The Hermetic Order of the Golden Dawn, for example, drew in men and women of intellect, including writers Arthur Machen and W. B. Yeats. Golden Dawn magic was officially 'white' but any magical beliefs can easily topple over into the pit of darkness and in many cases the pit was entered without the prior pretence of working *good* deeds through magical rituals.

I am not saying that there is genuine power in magic, whether Black, White or Khaki. On the contrary, I hold that all magical claims are nonsensical: it is self-delusion from start to finish. Even so, the direst nonsense can become a force when people believe in it. We only have to think of the racial teachings of the Nazis to provide a modern example.

The ideology of the Black practitioners has been described by Eliphas Levi in these words:

All must be dared in order to achieve all – such was the axiom of enchantments and their associated horrors. The false magicians were banded together by crime and believed that they could intimidate others when they had contrived to terrify themselves. The rites of Black Magic have remained revolting like the impious worships it produced; this was the case . . . in the association of criminals who conspired against the old civilisations and among the barbaric races. There was always the same passion for darkness; there were the same profanations, the same sanguin-

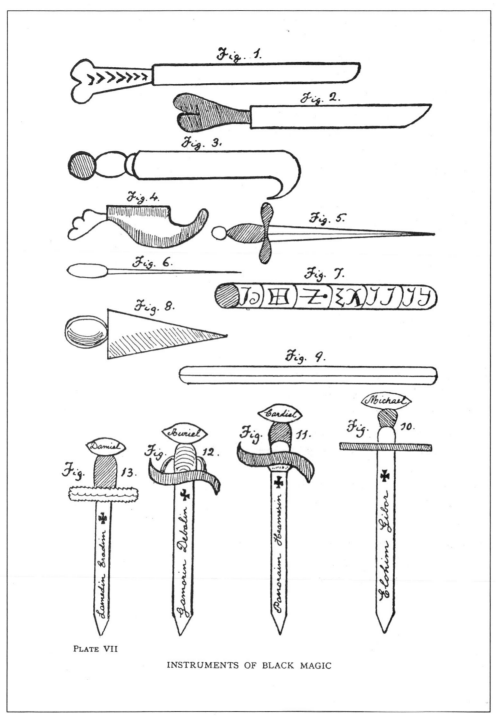

PLATE VII

INSTRUMENTS OF BLACK MAGIC

· The Black Art was obsessed with blood-letting.

ary processes. Anarchic Magic is the cultus of death. The sorcerer devotes himself to fatality, abjures reason, renounces the hope of immortality, and then sacrifices children. He forswears marriage and is given over to barren debauch. On such conditions he enjoys the plenitude of his mania, is made drunk with iniquity till he believes that evil is omnipotent and, converting his hallucinations into reality, he thinks that his mastery has power to evoke at pleasure all death and Hades.

Barbarian words and signs unknown, or even utterly unmeaning, are the best in Black Magic. Hallucination is insured more readily by ridiculous practices and imbecile evocations than by rites or formulae which keep intelligence in a waking state.

The driving force behind such crude rites and beliefs is always a warped sexual impulse: the terror and trembling tied in with the rites is overtly sexual. The Ripper harnessed all these potent forces – desire, hate, fear – to key up mind and body ready for the sexual slaughter on the streets. He became 'drunk with iniquity'. He came to believe that evil was omnipotent. He converted his hallucinations into reality.

In his December 1888 article in *The Gazette*, D'Onston reveals the satanic plan behind the killings. The sites were chosen beforehand. Each corpse was meant to lie along the lines of an imaginary cross straddling Whitechapel: in that way the supreme Christian symbol was profaned as the Black Art demanded. The bodies were mutilated to supply materials for future sordid rituals. The whole venture was foreshadowed by early teachings of the Satanists.

His confessional article was carefully rigged to look like the conclusions of an outside observer. It satisfied the need to boast and taunt and at the same time there was little chance of it being taken too seriously. The British public was convinced that such hideous activities could only take place in far-off foreign parts. Indeed, earlier that year these prejudices had been fortified by a report in the 21 April edition of *Cassell's Saturday Journal*. It read: 'An association, which is very properly known as the Diabolical Sect, is now flourishing in China . . . The sect is composed of fanatics who profess to believe that a sovereign cure for all the ills that flesh is heir to exists in the brains of young children . . . Their usual practice is to steal up noiselessly from behind, smash the child's head with a heavy club, and take out the brains with a shell . . .'

D'Onston employed other cunning tactics to shield himself. He talked about the murders to George Marsh, a would-be amateur detective. In priming Marsh, he named the killer as Dr Morgan Davies of the London

Hospital, but he spoke so realistically about the killings that he guessed Marsh would draw his own, very different conclusions. D'Onston proved to be an astute psychologist. Marsh brushed the Davies name to one side as a blatant decoy, then went to Scotland Yard and fingered Roslyn D'Onston as Jack the Ripper.

This development had been cunningly anticipated: two days after Marsh made his move, D'Onston went in person to the Yard and wrote out a long statement, repeating and amplifying his charges against Dr Davies. Missing papers prevent us from knowing the full sequel to this charade but there is little doubt that ultimately it served its purpose – it made D'Onston look like an obsessive time-waster, one not to be taken seriously. It also influenced police attitudes when he was arrested as the possible killer.

In 1890, just over a year after the last killing, a now frail D'Onston joined with novelist Mabel Collins and theosophist Vittoria Cremers in a short-lived business venture, The Pompadour Cosmetique Company, manufacturers of beauty creams and elixirs. During that year both women became convinced that D'Onston was quite capable of murder. His mistress, Mabel, came to live in terror after he convinced her that he was indeed the Ripper. She confided her fears to Cremers but would never go into full details, telling her only that it was 'something he said to me. Something he showed me. I cannot tell even you, but I know it, and I am afraid.' Her fear of saying more may have been implanted by magical threats uttered by D'Onston, for Mabel was a gullible believer in the power of magic, indeed she was even accused of using Black Magic precepts in her own writings.

Then D'Onston's capacity to terrorise ended dramatically. Like other guilt-tormented creatures before him, he underwent the profoundest of all changes – religious conversion. The man whose writings had all been concerned with murder, magic and necromancy, with never a word to say about Christianity, now became a devout Christian. Increasingly troubled by ill-health, sometimes partly paralysed, he spent years struggling over the text of his one book, a scholarly study of the Holy Gospels as they existed in the Second Century.

His *Patristic Gospels* was published in 1904 and shortly afterwards, his Christian mission completed, he simply disappeared from sight. His fate still remains an enigma.

What is it that makes Roslyn D'Onston such a certain suspect as Jack the Ripper? It is a combination of many things, past and present. In the

Arrested on suspicion,
never caught in the act,
D'Onston led a charmed life.

past we find no direct parallels to use for straightforward comparisons. At best we can take the cases of Dr Lamson and Dr Cream. Lamson was hanged for wife-poisoning in 1882. Before that he'd been a medical student in Paris, a volunteer with the French Ambulance Corps in 1870, and with the Red Cross in the Balkan uprising. He came from a good home but had acquired the morphine habit, with all its personality-twisting side-effects. After killing, he tried to hoodwink the police with false clues. He and D'Onston had a good deal in common.

In Cream's case we again have the good family background and the morphine addiction. After poisoning his prostitutes, Cream tried to pin the blame on another doctor and then on a medical student, very like D'Onston's tactic. And, like D'Onston, he sought out a detective with Scotland Yard and talked to him about the murders. Yet neither Lamson nor Cream had the degree of control and foresight exhibited by D'Onston.

Today we have far too much experience of the sexual serial-murderer, but that experience does provide knowledge. The Behavioural Science Unit of the FBI has systematically studied such killers and its findings show what we should look for. Someone normal-looking, intelligent, a pleasant person, even. Someone like an innocuous next-door neighbour, a man hard to suspect, if at all. There will be no signs of the rages within; the secret lives will stay submerged. Such killers, then, are very different from the old-fashioned stereotypes that once dominated popular and even police thought. They are certainly not the homicidal maniacs the police of 1888 were obsessed with.

One of these killers, Edmund Kemper, is well worth looking at. He killed girl after girl in the Santa Cruz area and the killings only came to an end when he turned himself in – having first despatched his mother.

I have listened to Kemper speak and watched his face. He comes across as a pleasant, quiet-spoken man; even the FBI men describe him as 'a nice guy'. And yet he went out seeking victims. In two cases he cut off the heads of the dead girls, operating in front of his own house, with his mother and neighbours at home. As he put it, he started flaunting his invisibility.

Kemper's calm exterior concealed the violent storms inside. He even hung out at a bar across the street from the Court House, making friends with the policemen who used it. He talked to the officers about the murders and they came to regard him as a friendly nuisance. 'It was deliberate,' says Kemper. 'Friendly nuisances are dismissed.' How right he was. But D'Onston had shown this a century earlier. When he'd gone to the Yard in 1888 he confided his tale to Inspector Roots, a detective he'd known, on and off, for twenty years. The inspector had good reason to doubt the value of the story; even so, as his report shows, he still stayed impressed by D'Onston, despite this new role as a friendly nuisance.

Like Kemper, D'Onston was soft-spoken, courteous, disarming. He was also adept at flaunting his invisibility. Unlike Kemper, though, he had a sharp intellect, nerves of steel and an ideology which helped him rationalise his inhuman impulses. What's more, he was no stranger to killing. Sword in hand, he had killed legitimately on the battlefields of Italy. At the impressionable age of eighteen, he had become hardened to the sight of blood, death and mutilation.

In 1888 he was living in Whitechapel, aware of all its myriad back streets, alleys and courts. His retentive mind missed nothing that would be of use, when the time came. As a journalist he could legitimately prowl around at all hours in search of copy. His gentle, calm front would allow him to talk sympathetically to any street-walker.

The prostitutes were naturally the easiest victims to choose. In addition, the harlot always played an important role in the arcana of Black Magic. But did the memory of long-lost Ada play its part as well? Did he blame harlotry for the death of his love-affair and the death of the loved one? Was her suicide laid at the feet of the whole profession? Very probably, for few ideologies stay immutable. They become mixed in with other ideas quite readily, thus the magical theories could easily inter-twine with personal grievances. So revenge, resentment and repression all united to create the inward rage and the public terror.

Despite his cunning and diversions, he still failed to deceive everyone. George Marsh certainly saw through him, yet D'Onston would have smiled at that. But he underestimated the astuteness of *Gazette* editor, W. T. Stead. D'Onston spoke to, and wrote to, Stead about the murders and Stead came to regard him in a very new light. Undoubtedly D'Onston gave too much away in his confidences, for years later, in 1896, Stead wrote this of him: 'He has been known to me for many years. He is one of the most remarkable persons I ever met. For more than a year I was under the impression that he was the veritable Jack the Ripper; an impression which I believe was shared by the police, who at least once, had him under arrest; although, as he completely satisfied them, they liberated him without bringing him into court.'

TO SPORTSMEN, TOURISTS, & TRAVELLERS.

EDMISTON'S POCKET SIPHONIA,

OR WATERPROOF OVERCOAT.

WEIGHT 10 oz.

Sole Manufacturers of the celebrated Pocket Siphonia, remarkable for its lightness and softness of texture, adapted for Sportsmen, Travellers, and Tourists, easily folded to carry in the Pocket or on Saddle ; the most *important* feature in this *Waterproofing* is being mineralised, which effectually resists the powerful heat of the sun and the most violent rains, also obviating the stickiness and unpleasant smell peculiar to all other Waterproofs.—Price according to size, 40s. to 55s. ; all silk throughout, 50s. to 65s. Measurement, length of coat, and size round the chest over the coat.

NOTICE.—NAME & ADDRESS STAMPED INSIDE. NONE OTHERS ARE GENUINE.

EDMISTON & SON, WATERPROOFERS, 416, STRAND,

Near the Adelphi Theatre.

THE VERSATIO,

OR REVERSIBLE COAT.

WORTHY THE ATTENTION OF THE NOBLEMAN, MERCHANT, OR TRADESMAN.

No. 1.   Reversed.

The importance of this *patented* invention consists in the novelty of the material and its application, viz., the double purpose of forming two in one without trouble, one side presenting a gentlemanly morning coat, the other a riding, shooting, or hunting coat, in any texture or colour desired.

In over-garments or paletots this happy discovery offers still more useful advantages to the wearer, one surface exhibiting a graceful and elegant walking coat, while its counterpart is conveniently adapted for the rougher purposes of travelling, skilfully designed in each, and perfect in both their capacities. In these varying properties the public must recognise an union of novelty and usefulness not hitherto accomplished. Gentlemen supplied sending their height and size round the chest over the waistcoat. Price from 50s. to 70s.

LONDON : EDMISTON & SON, TAILORS, 69, STRAND, opposite the Adelphi Theatre.

Bloodstains were no problem for a canny killer. Reversible coats
had been on sale for many years.

These words are well worth dwelling on. D'Onston lowered his guard with Stead and said just a little too much. Stead, in turn, began to probe and came to see things in D'Onston's character and behaviour that showed him capable of murder. And not just ordinary murder, but the bizarre knife-killings that were the hallmark of the Ripper. This conviction stayed with Stead for over a year and made such an impression on him that eight years later he felt impelled to record it.

What caused Stead to abandon his view? Since no one ever asked him, we have to guess at the reason and it probably stems from the idea that the Ripper went on killing *after* 1888. This belief was held by many newspapers and even Police Commissioner Monro was uncertain. Monro at first saw the McKenzie murder of July 1889 as 'identical with the notorious Jack the Ripper of last year'. Two months later came the finding of the body under the railway arch, and again Monro speculated that it might be another Ripper victim. Given this confusion, it is likely that D'Onston had an unbreakable alibi for the time of one of the pseudo-Ripper events, and that was enough for Stead to back down.

'There will be no more murders,' said D'Onston in July 1890. By then he was incapable of fresh terror escapades. Following the Kelly murder, he suffered a breakdown in health and was bedridden in the London Hospital, Whitechapel. Just weeks after discharge he was back in hospital once more, and the old stamina never returned. In the end his new-found faith protected him from the dark, deadly passions within him. We may not know how and when D'Onston died, but this much is certain: the Ripper died the moment D'Onston was born again.

W. T. Stead saw D'Onston as the Ripper.

Epilogue

We have no cause to feel complacent. A century later, the twisted faith the Ripper embraced lives on. On 13 April 1989 newspapers throughout the world carried a chilling story from the United States. One headline read: SATAN MONSTERS STAKED SCREAMING VICTIMS TO ALTAR. One column ran: 'Devil-worshipping drug smugglers butchered and ATE at least twelve people in horrific moonlit ceremonies . . . Screaming victims – who had been kidnapped at random – were staked to a crude altar and savagely tortured. The crazed satanists then chopped them up, tore out their hearts and sucked out their brains . . .'

This horror was staged at a ranch in Mexico, just over the border from the USA. Police Lieutenant Gavito explained that the cult turned cannibal to please the devil. Their human sacrifices were to gain power 'so the police would not arrest them, so bullets would not kill them and so they could make more money'.

Appendix

Joseph Sickert is a painter with a head full of marvellous dreams. He insists that the renowned artist, Walter Sickert, was his father. He further claims that Prince Albert Victor, Duke of Clarence, was his grandfather. In themselves these unlikely claims are harmless enough, but in 1972 Joseph Sickert allowed his fantasies to swirl out of control and the damage began.

He evolved a lurid tale encompassing his grandmother, the Duke of Clarence and Jack the Ripper. At the time, there was a revival of interest in the possible identity of the Ripper and this inspired the BBC to plan a television series on the murders. Among the theories picked up by BBC researchers was that advanced by Sickert. They looked into it, but not exhaustively enough, and drew a false conclusion: they imagined that they were faced with a theory that had some substance to it. Along the way they had missed the essential clues that would have warned them that the truth was being mangled.

In August 1973 Joseph Sickert appeared in the last programme of the BBC six-part *Jack the Ripper* series. On screen he stated that the murders had been committed in order to protect the Royal Family. The liaison between his grandmother and the Duke of Clarence had led to a secret marriage and the birth of a daughter. If these transgressions became known to the public, then the consequences would be dire, for '. . . it was a time when the possibility of revolution was thought to be a very real one'. So a cover-up operation became a priority.

The Duke's bride, Annie Crook, was effectively silenced by being certified as insane, but the couple's servant, Mary Kelly, fled into the slums of Whitechapel and there she nursed her dangerous knowledge, until the knifeman caught up with her. But why were the others killed? As a diversion, explained Sickert, to baffle the public and draw attention away from the only victim who really mattered.

Who was it then, who cut and carved his way into criminal history? It was none other, said Sickert, than Sir William Gull, the royal physician, aided by a coachman named John Netley.

These grotesque assertions should have been quietly laid to rest within days. Well-directed research would have killed off this nonsense for good, but the opportunity was missed and the story fell into the hands of the late Stephen Knight who gave it a fake pedigree.

In Knight's hands the story was enlarged into book form and tricked out with 'documentation' which seemed to give it substance. But it was just so much clever deception, from start to finish, a deception that has been fully exposed in my book *Jack the Ripper: The Bloody Truth*. Thus there is no longer any excuse left for *anyone* to present the Gull story as truth. But if you give a lie a head-start then the truth often has difficulty in overtaking it.

Until 1988 Knight's book served as the inspiration for a number of works that were openly fictional. Even so, because they all harked back to a 'factual source', they helped the spread of the Gull hoax. The most influential of these works was a novel, *The Night Of The Ripper*, by Robert Bloch, author of *Psycho*.

Bloch's career had been dramatically altered by an earlier brush with the Ripper. A 1943 story of his, *Yours Truly, Jack the Ripper*, caught on in the USA and was dramatised for radio on four different shows. Its text caught the eye of Alfred Hitchcock and ultimately led to the production of *Psycho*. Little wonder, then, that Bloch has read everything ever written on the Whitechapel killings, and he shows this in his novel. But for a fuller dramatic line he builds up two minor characters, neither of whom played any part in the real Ripper hunt. These are actor Richard Mansfield, famous for his duel role in *Jekyll and Hyde*, and spiritualist Robert James Lees. In addition, he casts the coachman, Netley, as the man who takes the Duke of Clarence whoring in White-chapel – all new touches worth remembering.

When it came to new touches, though, no one could out-master film-maker David Wickes. In September 1987 the world suddenly learned that Mr Wickes had discovered the true identity of the killer through studying files *unseen by anyone else*. In a press release from his London office at Queen's Gate, he later said:

> Scores of dossiers were compiled . . . yet all these files remain closed to the public . . . The secret files on Jack the Ripper have never been made available to anyone. Until now. After several years of trying, David Wickes Productions Ltd. finally gained access to the files of the Home

Office and the Metropolitan Police last year . . . the secret Home Office and Metropolitan Police Files have always remained closed. Until now.

Now the claims made by Mr Wickes were not only arrogant but were impermissibly false as well. This was confirmed at once by the Home Office. The facts are that the complete files on the murders were made available to Stephen Knight as long ago as 1975. Since then, as the Home Office states:

> Prior to the opening to public inspection at the Public Record Office of the Home Office files on the Whitechapel murders, privileged access was allowed to all bona fide researchers. No exclusive access has been allowed to these files to any one researcher, nor are there any secret Home Office files on the murders. (Letter to the author, 9 November 1987.)

The Home Office statement surely demanded an immediate withdrawal of the spurious claims, yet this never happened. The reason? An expensive television deal was in the offing and 'the secret files' formed part of the sales package. This was admitted by Leslie Moonves, senior vice-president of the American-based production company, Lorimar. He had made a co-production deal with Wickes's English backers, Thames Television, stated to be worth over £4.5 million. When Max Pragnell of *The Sunday Times* spoke to Moonves and asked about the deal, Moonves replied: 'The deal may not have gone ahead without Wickes's access to the files. He maintained all along that we had them to ourselves. Of course, we may have got involved anyway . . . but those files were the real clincher. For the moment we'll have to stick with Thames.'

That revealing interview was published on 6 March 1988 but it took a further three months before Ross Benson was able to report: 'There has been a shame-faced climb-down by the makers of the forthcoming Jack the Ripper film, following my disclosure that Thames TV were making less than truthful claims about the production. It was on the basis that hitherto unreleased Scotland Yard files had been made available that the £4,500,000 film . . . was sold to the Americans. But, as I revealed, there are no new files. Now producer David Wickes has had to bite the bullet and admit as much. "There are no secret files," he says, blaming over-zealous publicists for the hype . . . This retreat is too late to save the Americans, however. Lorimar had bought the film before the truth was known.' (*The Daily Express*, 9 June 1988.)

When the completed film was finally screened the full extent of the grand bluff became clear: all the boasted-of research had yielded up nothing new. The millions had been spent to perpetuate folly. The promised devastating solution was simply the Gull hoax once again. An innocent man was once more recklessly smeared.

There was a sense of *déjà vu* about the film. It looked like an over-the-top hybrid between Bloch's novel and Knight's *Final Solution*. On screen we saw Lees and Mansfield and their imaginary involvements, while coachman Netley obliged by carrying the Duke to the whores and Gull to the shambles. It was an affront to every viewer who had been waiting for an authentic solution. It was an affront compounded by a screened statement that read: 'We have come to our conclusions after careful study and painstaking deduction.'

Just minutes away from the Thames studios lives the man who knows that 'careful study and painstaking deduction' can never lead to Sir William Gull or to Netley. Their involvement in murder is imaginary. Even their involvement with each other is imaginary. He knows this for certain for he invented the wretched hoax. He has publicly admitted that there is no truth in it and all competent research confirms this. Until he named Gull and Netley as partners in the killings no one *anywhere* had ever dreamed of such a deadly alliance. Joseph Sickert certainly has a lot to answer for, but at least he has had the courage to own up to his deceit.

As things stand, an honourable man and an outstanding physician has been branded a killer. The fantasies of a self-confessed liar have been given credence and large numbers of the public have been unwittingly duped. Does the search for profits justify this? This is a question that has to be squarely faced by Thames Television. It is an issue not to be evaded, for ultimately it involves accountability and integrity and no media company can afford to raise doubts on those scores – not even a rich one.

Note on Bibliography

The D'Onston documentation, including the Scotland Yard papers, can be found in the last chapter of my book *Jack the Ripper: The Bloody Truth*; and a list of his writings is included in the bibliography to that book. When reading anything by D'Onston, bear in mind that it will be distorted by two factors. In the first place there was his need to talk about his past, while concealing his real name and family connections. Secondly, he believed that he had significant things to say – but only to the worthy – so he rather conceitedly decided to make use of oblique parables, imitating the techniques of the much-admired Lytton. In speaking of a proposed book of his he said: '. . . readers will have to decide for themselves how much is absolute matter of fact – whether all or none – and how much imagination. It will not be my part to give any clue to the student of occultism; it may convey many new ideas and indicate the true lines on which his investigations should proceed . . .'

It should also be noted that all references to D'Onston in works prior to mine should be disregarded. The earlier material is grossly inaccurate and has now been superseded. Any pieces on D'Onston written by Aleister Crowley should be read for their curiosity value only, and not taken seriously.

D'Onston's Customs Service records can be found at the Public Record Office at Kew. To date he has only been located in one Census Return, that for Kingston upon Hull of 1861. On that return he is shown as living with his family in Sculcoates. Under 'Rank, Profession, or Occupation' he is recorded as 'Lieutenant Southern Army Italy, Retired'.

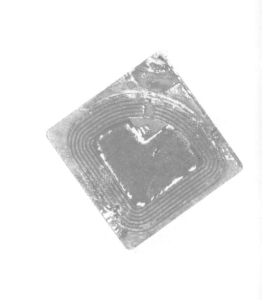